White House Pets

White House Pets

by

MARGARET TRUMAN

DAVID McKAY COMPANY, INC.

New York

WHITE HOUSE PETS

Library of Congress Catalog Card Number: 68-29633

MANUFACTURED IN THE UNITED STATES OF AMERICA

VAN REES PRESS • NEW YORK

ACKNOWLEDGMENTS

My appreciation to those who helped with the research for this book, especially to Howard Liss and to the two ladies, Mrs. Robert Land and Mrs. Herbert Sanborne, who located the pictures through the Library of Congress, one of the great institutions of this country.

My thanks to Mr. James R. Ketchum, Curator of the White House, who has answered many queries, always with great patience.

CONTENTS

LIST OF ILLUSTRATIONS

(following page 52)

LIST OF ILLUSTRATIONS

(following page 116)

White House Pets

Chapter 1

THEY ALL LIVED TOGETHER

THERE really is no difference between a White House pet and yours or mine except that those belonging to our Chief Executive receive more publicity. But that is one of the hazards the President's pets must face—it comes with the office.

Of those taking up residence at the White House or a Presidential summer home, some arrive with their distinguished masters or are purchased shortly after the First Families are comfortably settled. Others are gifts from friends, well-wishers, or foreign officials.

We will try to tell about a great many of them, from George Washington's horse Nelson, who was at the surrender at Yorktown, to the one-day news item about my father's white puppy that I don't even remember.

In all these stories of President's pets it is apparent that, though most of the animals may have been ordinary, their masters were not. The office they held is complex beyond comprehension, with responsibilities so overwhelming that even Presidents themselves cannot describe them adequately. If animals gave them a moment's relaxation or a short respite from continual burdens, then I think they're worth remembering for that reason if for no other.

George Washington, our first President, was also the first to receive gift pets. Admirers sent him some fine hunting dogs; from the king of Spain came a champion jack that he kept at Mount Vernon for many years. It should be remembered, of course, that Washington never lived in the White House, which was not completed until 1800.

A pet need not live within the confines of the White House in order to be officially considered a pet. There are eighteen acres of grounds around the White House and there are plenty of squirrels living among the trees. I shall tell a story about a wild rabbit—though I never saw one there myself.

In good weather, my family liked to eat on the South Portico. We took almost all our meals there during the late spring and summer months. It was pleasant, airy, and allowed my father a brief hour of relaxation in the sunshine. Sometimes we noticed a group of squirrels chasing around close to the porch. Our table was a marvelous glass-topped rectangular one, with a ring attached to the legs, where a bowl of fresh flowers could be placed that could be seen through the table top. It gave a very pretty effect. One day we caught Dad crumbling soda crackers by his chair where, he thought, his actions were hidden by the flower bowl under the glass top. No wonder we had so many squirrel visitors. Mother allowed as how she'd prefer no more wild visitors under the table at lunch. Who wants to be bitten by a squirrel? Dad agreed but then fed them at the edge of the porch after lunch. The Trumans are stubborn that way.

As President Theodore Roosevelt and others have pointed out, birds too find the White House an attractive place. Sometimes these wild creatures can present a baffling problem to the White House staff. During World War I, for example, attendants and guards were startled to hear a loud, distinct tapping one night. Its point of origin was unknown. This was a time of rumors, of spies under every bed, with plots, counterplots, and scare stories manufactured as fast as the imagination could conceive them. The tapping noise was finally tracked down when an attendant went up on the roof to get some air and happened to look in the right direction at the right time. It was a woodpecker hammering away at the copper gutters and down-spouts. When the woodpecker was gone, so was the tapping.

Two of the most unusual cases of odd animals staying at the White House occurred during the administrations of John Quincy Adams and Andrew Johnson. Mr. Adams was quite an intellectual. From listening to him one would never guess his farm background, for he spoke mostly about science, literature, and history. State dinners given by Mr. Adams were on the dull side. Some of the most interesting guests were reduced to simple pleasantries. Such excitement as there was came from visiting dignitaries.

General Lafayette had been touring the United States from July 1824 to August 1825, and spent his last two months of his trip in the White House. Among the many gifts he had received was a live alligator, which he kept in the East Room. Frequently visitors who wandered in came tearing out again—fast.

Mrs. John Quincy Adams also kept unusual "pets": silkworms who feasted on mulberry leaves and repaid their hostess by spinning the silk for the First Lady's dresses. I find that hard to believe, but it's supposed to be true.

As for Andrew Johnson, one summer evening with the air of a conspirator he showed his favorite secretary, one Mr. Moore, a bushel basket of flour, which came from one of the mills he owned at Greenville, Tenn. He explained that the night before he had found a few mice playing, and in a fit of generosity he had left a handful of flour for the scurrying little beasts.

"I am now filling the basket for them tonight," the President said. The next day Moore asked the President about his tiny friends.

"The little fellows gave me their confidence," the President answered. "I gave them their basket and poured some water [into a bowl] on the hearth for them."

For the average family, the word pet means dogs, cats, canaries, parakeets, hamsters, and in cases where a stable permits, horses or ponies. Generally, the same holds true for our First Family, except that their lofty position leaves them exposed to gifts that no family in its right mind would contemplate for even an instant. Would the typical suburbanite accept an elephant as a present? Or a zebra? A pair of frisky, sharp-toothed lion cubs? A vicious bobcat? A baby hippo?

Well, at various times, several of our Presidents, including Martin Van Buren, Theodore Roosevelt, and Calvin Coolidge, have been notified that a friend, a foreign potentate, or government official was giving such a beast to the White House as a token of esteem. Presidents, being politicians, usually make a show of appreciation at the thoughtfulness of the donor. Then they ship the animals to the nearest zoo, which in the case of Washington, D.C., happens to be the Washington Zoo on Connecticut Avenue.

Another problem that must be faced by White House tenants is accommodations. Many homes boast a good-sized doghouse in the backyard; apartment dwellers allow their pets a corner of some room or even the freedom to roam as they wish. That is often the case in the White House. But cats and dogs arrive constantly, and as pets begin to pile up they must be quartered somewhere on the grounds.

Years before the Presidential mansion was called the

White House, Presidents kept animals, usually horses and dogs. Washington had both carriage and hunting horses in stables at the Presidential residences, in the capitals located in New York City and Philadelphia and at his home, Mount Vernon.

The President's House in Washington was begun in 1792, but the second President, John Adams, could not move from the Philadelphia capital to Washington until 1800. When he arrived, he found a still unfurnished President's House in a crude settlement along the Potomac, and he didn't move in until November.

But the land was beautiful and Adams, a farmer at heart, said in one of his letters to his wife Abigail: "I wish I had a farm here." His own farm in Quincy, Massachusetts, was named "Peacefield"; Washington, D.C., must have seemed a lovely, serene place in those days.

It was still a backwater small town when John Adams's grandson, John Quincy Adams, became President. John Quincy was a great swimmer. At the age of sixty he boasted he could swim a mile across the Potomac in an hour and he was capable of doing just that. During the hot summer months, come sunrise, Mr. Adams was on the banks of the river stripping off his clothes and plunging in. According to my father he was caught one day by a lady reporter who wanted an interview. She stole his clothes while he was swimming and refused to give them back until he granted the interview.

For President John Adams's horses in Washington, a stable was constructed, located in the square block that is now bounded by F and G and 13th and 14th Streets. The brick structure contained stalls for twelve horses, the carriage house accommodated three carriages, and a small room held grain. It was built by one William Lovell at a cost of $1600. From then on, there was no end of trouble over the location of later stables built at the expense of the United States Government.

President Jefferson evidently did not like the location of the Adamses' stables for he had new ones built as well as a cowshed and carriage house. The abandoned Adams stables were remodeled and used as a private school. After former pupils and souvenir hunters vandalized it, the structure went through other alterations. Half a century later this building was sold and became a carpenter shop. Today a bank stands on the original site.

In 1806, Jefferson built his stables on the west side of the White House. In 1814, the invading British leveled them. At the same time the President's House was gutted (for the first time) by a fire set by the British, and only the outer shell was left standing. When restored, the outer walls were painted white to cover the blackened stone—thus it became known as the White House.

During my father's administration, the White House had become so rickety that it was gutted and restored once more, to keep us from sliding into the basement.

After the fire in 1814, there were no proper stables, just

7

makeshift ones in various locations around the White House, until Andrew Jackson's second term, when a permanent structure was built. This was removed to make way for enlarging the Treasury and another built in 1857. These stables burned in 1864 during Lincoln's term. They were again rebuilt by President Grant, but did not serve long, being torn down in 1871 and replaced by a handsome two-story red brick building with a mansard roof, located opposite the Corcoran Gallery of Art. They were converted into a garage in 1909 by President Taft, who owned no less than a White Steamer, two Pierce Arrows, and a Baker Electric. They shared the garage-stables with the famous Taft cow, Pauline. When the stables were torn down in 1911 and the new President's garage was built at 19th and B Streets, Pauline moved with the elegant cars to the new building. But she came home to "graze on those exclusive preserves" as the *Evening Star* reported. "She is led there in a dewy morning and taken away in the twilight . . ."

As for horses, before the twentieth century all Presidents owned some. Horses served as transportation, both for the saddle, and to draw a coach or carriage. Presidents, like all people who owned horses, set great store by their favorite steeds. When John Tyler's horse died, the President buried him at Sherwood, Charles City County, Virginia, with the inscription, "Here lies the body of my good horse, The General. For years he bore me around the circuit of my practice and all that time he never made a

8

blunder. Would that his master could say the same—John Tyler." Thus did one of my Truman ancestors honor his horse.

President James Garfield kept horses for himself and his family. His little daughter Molly especially liked to ride. At least she did at the beginning. Her favorite was a brown mare named Kit. According to the custom in those days she rode sidesaddle. One day a stable hand failed to tighten the girth properly and while Molly was aboard Kit, the saddle slipped and tilted. The horse shied and bolted. Molly was thrown to the ground, but one foot was caught in the stirrup. For a few moments the screaming child was dragged around until the horse was caught by the bridle and Molly was released. Had someone told the youngster to get right back in the saddle, everything would have been all right, for Molly was unharmed. But nobody did, and Molly never rode again.

Dogs were the White House staple as far as pets were concerned. Through the years, kennels have been scattered in a number of places on the White House grounds. Sometimes special buildings were hastily erected to house them. On occasion a spare room at ground level, such as the Flower Room, was pressed into service as quarters for dogs. Favored dogs were allowed to roam about, at times sleeping in the bedroom of their master or mistress.

One of the most fetching dogs ever to adorn the White House scene was a small spaniel belonging to Maria Hester Monroe, daughter of President James Monroe. Maria was fourteen years old when her father assumed the office of President, but long before that, her ethereal beauty was the talk of the capital. Mrs. Monroe took great pains with the little girl's education and dressed her in the latest little girl's Paris creations. Judge Henry St. George Tucker of Virginia, a friend of the Monroe's, was so smitten with Maria Hester that he wrote a letter to his own daughter describing the girl and her clothing, so that the Judge's granddaughter might present a similar appearance. According to a volume published by the University of North Carolina Press, Judge Tucker wrote: "Your Mama has referred you to me for an account of little Maria Monroe who is I believe a few months older than our darling Francilea. She was dressed in a short frock that reached about halfway between her ankles and knees, under which she displayed a pair of loose pantaloons wide enough for the foot to pass through with ease, frilled around with the same stuff as her frock and pantaloons. The little monkey did not fail to evince the advantage of her dress." Then referring to the pet in favor at the moment, the Judge added, "She had a small spaniel dog with whom she was continually engaged in a trial of skill and the general opinion seemed to be that she turned and twisted about more than the spaniel. I must recommend her dress for my dear brats." *

According to an item in the *Washington Star* dated No-

* William Cresson, *James Monroe* (Chapel Hill: University of North Carolina Press, 1946). Reprinted by permission.

vember 22, 1895, Mrs. Grover Cleveland received a nine-month-old, 1½-pound, black Japanese poodle. The dog, a gift from a Milwaukee man, August C. Klavel, was described as being the smallest pug dog in the United States. Obviously some mistake was made. Was it a poodle or a pug? Nobody is quite sure to this day, but in all likelihood it was neither. Probably it was a Pekingese and not from Japan but China.

Friends of the President have a problem: what gift does one present to the daughter of a President of the United States? The safest is a pet. One fine day when I came home from school, I found that Bob Hannigan, the Postmaster General, had presented me with an Irish setter puppy. I named him Mike—what else can you name an Irish setter given to you by a man named Hannigan?

Mike was our only pet—Dad could take or leave pets—and Mike developed into quite a dog—physically, that is. However, he never outgrew being a puppy. On numerous occasions I'd sit in a porch chair and promptly find myself covered with a lapful of dog. Mike had no compunction about leaping onto me whenever the opportunity presented itself.

Once Mike jumped into the garden pool and my mother's secretary, Reathel Odum, jumped in to pull him out. Reathel, knowing nothing about dogs, didn't realize he could swim. Result: one soaked, mad secretary, one soaked, delighted dog.

Mike wouldn't come when I called. I was chasing after him once, just at dusk, and going along below the South Portico, I came upon a window. The shade was up and bright lights revealed that inside the room the walls were covered with maps. I looked in, and recognized one of my father's aides, one of the younger ones, and waved. All the aides waved back rather nervously, and immediately rushed to pull the shade down. I caught Mike and went off, not thinking much about it until I remembered that there was a secret map room in the White House. This was early in 1945. I had discovered where the map room was, and only a few people besides my father were supposed to know—not even the people who worked in the White House every day. I mentioned it to my father the next day at breakfast, and he told me just to keep quiet about that and not tell anybody where it was.

Mike's problems were compounded by the White House police. They kept feeding him candy. Since the setter couldn't refuse a handout, and ate anything and everything, in a short time poor Mike developed a case of rickets. He was cured soon enough, but I realized that Mike would be better off in someone else's hands. He was given to a man in Virginia who raised bird dogs. I learned later that he was quite happy in his new home.

President Eisenhower was quite fond of dogs and always had one or two about, even while he was European wartime chief. Then he had a black Scotty named Spunky who strongly resembled President Roosevelt's Fala. He gave this dog to his son John. One of his favorites, given to him while he was President, was a brownish Weimaraner named Heidi. Weimaraners are an interesting breed, originally bred in Germany some 700 years ago as hunting dogs.

The President was quite taken with this one, so much so that he insisted on feeding her himself. Mostly Heidi remained at Gettysburg, the Eisenhowers' residence near Washington. She didn't enjoy Washington with all the hubbub of noise, and people always in her way.

For some reason Heidi didn't like to see Mrs. Eisenhower photographed. She would jump on the First Lady whenever she as much as saw a camera. Nor was she overly friendly with Spunky. When Spunky visited with Grandson David, Heidi was banished to the third floor of the White House. That wasn't much of a hardship, for there she would find Sergeant Moaney, one of the President's staff. In fact, whenever President Eisenhower wanted to send the dog off for awhile, he would simply tell her to go find Moaney, and Heidi usually did.

Richard Nixon's Checkers, the lovable, floppy-eared cocker spaniel, who was a *cause célèbre* in the 1952 election, has since been replaced by a stunning six-month-old Irish setter named King Timahoe presented to Nixon by his staff. The new dog's bloodline is impeccable: his forebears are champions.

Daughter Julie has a cuddlesome poodle named Vicky,

and her sister Tricia owns a cute Yorkshire terrier she calls Pasha. The latter dog joined the Nixon household because both girls seem to know the secret of getting around their father. When Tricia asked for Pasha, she had fallen in love with the little Yorkshire at first sight. Mrs. Nixon had her doubts, but the President promptly said *yes* to her plea, which only proves that Richard Nixon is the typical father where daughters are concerned.

Kittens and cats have sometimes enlivened the White House scene. In the case of one President, either he or a kitten had to go. The feline was called Tom Kitten, the President—JFK. There are several stories about cats such as Slippers and the diplomats, Tom Quartz and his feud with a dog, and the Lincolns' kittens.

Numerous Presidents and their First Ladies were fond of keeping canaries, parrots, mockingbirds, and other species. Thomas Jefferson's mockingbird was his constant companion. President Grover Cleveland's wife also had a mockingbird, as well as several canaries. Unlike Mr. Jefferson, Mr. Cleveland found the birds annoying on occasion, especially the mockingbird. One evening when he was up late working, the mockingbird's antics kept interrupting his concentration. He had the bird moved. Sudden silence and the fact that the bird might have been placed in a draft worried him even more. Mr. Pendel, an aide, spent part of the night moving the bird from place to place trying to find a compromise area where the mockingbird wouldn't catch cold, and where its warbling could not be heard by the President.

A friend sent a talking parrot to President McKinley. The exact species is obscure but a newspaper article printed in the *Washington Star* described it as a "Mexican double-yellow-headed parrot." It must have been a remarkable bird, for it was reportedly worth several thousand dollars.

President McKinley thought highly of this parrot, remarking that it was the most intelligent bird he had seen. "That parrot could complete almost any ordinary song I'd hum, sing or whistle," McKinley said. "If I began a few bars of Yankee Doodle or America, and then stopped, the parrot would finish the song."

From all reports the bird was truly a rare one, gifted with political savvy that would have done credit to a veteran vote-getter. When a group of women, young or old, middle-aged or better, would pass his cage, he would cock his head and screech, "Oh, look at all the pretty girls!"

There never has been any such thing as the typical or the most popular White House pet. Presidential favorites have varied with their personalities and families. Up until the administration of President Taft, cows were usually a part of the White House background. There were no dairy companies to deliver fresh milk in those early days so cows were practical as well as gentle pets for children.

In the White House basement where the winter fuel supply was kept, one could see the remains of marble vats set in the concrete floor. These home dairy containers were used to cool and store milk; cream was skimmed off with a special ladle and served as coffee cream, ice cream, and whipped cream.

It must also be remembered that Washington, D.C., was for a very long time simply a large cluster of houses and streets in a rural setting. Since the Chief Executives were familiar with farm life, it was quite normal to keep cows somewhere in the vicinity. President Rutherford B. Hayes was quite proud of his pedigreed Jersey cows. He also kept chickens, and so did Theodore Roosevelt and others. Andrew Johnson, whose heart had never really left the farming country of Tennessee, was a great milk drinker. His daughter Martha rose before sunrise to supervise the milking.

William Howard Taft was the last President to keep a cow. Pauline, a handsome Holstein, had as her pasture the grassy area behind the State War and Navy building. A handsome photograph of her in front of the ornate structure became famous.

Goats also came into their share of popularity. President Benjamin Harrison remembering his own goat cart rides of the past provided a similar rig for his grandchildren, just as his grandfather President William Henry Harrison had done for him. And we find President Rutherford B.

Hayes describing his son's activity in a letter with these words: "Scott's new goat is a success—he hauls Scott all about. The two dogs suit him too. Your mother's cat, dog, and mockingbird give a Robinson Crusoe touch to our mode of life."

Many White House pets defy all categories, but they provided good news copy in their day. One was a horned toad, another a green snake, a third was a kangaroo rat.

Some White House families stand out because of the number of pets they had—some kept very few. It's all a part of this very personal look into their histories.

Chapter 2

TEDDY ROOSEVELT'S ZOO

M UCH has been made of the fact that the former Rough Rider was a hunter. Those who abhor such taking of life point out the inconsistencies of his character. How can a man claim to love animals when he kills them? He didn't hunt for food which might have made it excusable. The man was simply chasing a beast and dropping it with a well-aimed shot. That was true enough, and there wasn't much Theodore Roosevelt could do to make his critics understand. Nor did he try.

Other people defended his hunting by pointing out that many Presidents liked to fish, and that there is very little difference between luring and hooking a fish and stalking and shooting a moose. Besides, Roosevelt never killed merely for the sake of killing. To him it was the chase that mattered. Only once did he depart from that course. When he was only seventeen years old, he killed his first deer in the Adirondack Mountains by "jacking." He built a fire in a container in the stern of his boat, attracted the beast, and lured it into rifle range. Roosevelt regretted it almost instantly. There had been no chase, no tracking, no practice of one of man's oldest instincts, the hunt. He never did that again.

Actually Theodore Roosevelt was one of the foremost naturalists of his time, and most of his knowledge was the result of first-hand observation. A Roosevelt stroll through groves, fields, and lawns was not simply for exercise. He looked, he listened, and he saw things that would have escaped the untutored eye.

His knowledge of birds was incredible. The President had no difficulty identifying even the most obscure species. Once he recorded what he had seen in his diary:

"A pair of red-headed woodpeckers that nested for three years in the White House grounds, while a mockingbird is to be found in several places within easy walking distance, although, sorry to say, it is not in the White House grounds. Neither is the Woodthrush, but it is abundant in Rock Creek Park within the city limits. Robins, song sparrows, crows, black birds nest in the ground. Crows, the enemy of all birds, are as such entitled to no mercy. The hearty wholesome songs of the Robins and the sweet homelike strains of the Song Sparrows are the first to be heard regularly in the ground and they lead the chorus. Two or three pairs of Flickers nest with us, and a pair of furtive Cuckoos. A pair of Orchard Orioles nested with us one spring, but not again. The Redstarts, Warbling Vireos, and Summer Warblers have been more faithful.

Baltimore Orioles visit us frequently, and so do the Scarlet Tanagers and Tufted Titmice. But for some reason they do not nest here."

Other references to birds are found throughout his notes and diaries. He often brought up the subject of winged visitors during casual conversation. One spring, to his great delight, the President was awakened almost every morning by a cardinal singing in a magnolia tree that stood just outside his bedroom. And that famous broad toothy grin brightened his face when he found a Carolina Wren singing in winter on the White House grounds. He would stop everything and listen, enthralled, as White Throated Sparrows would serenade with their fall and winter migrations.

Roosevelt was constantly on the lookout for Fox Sparrows, Tree Sparrows, and Snow Birds. On hot June days and nights he liked to sit on the South Portico of the White House and listen to the chanting of the Indigo Birds, or the soft calling of two small owls. He instilled this appreciation of nature in all his children. They were encouraged to fondle and pet any animal, except, of course, those that were poisonous or otherwise dangerous.

Some of the creatures the Roosevelt children chose as pets were a trifle on the exotic side.

For example, Alice Roosevelt liked snakes. One of her special favorites was a green snake she named Emily Spinach, partly because her Aunt Emily was very thin and partly because spinach is green. Once Alice took Emily

Spinach with her when visiting some friends. Suddenly
the snake disappeared behind the living room curtains.
Finally it was found in another room where it had shed
its skin. It is the story of Quentin and the snakes that will
be remembered as long as the antics of small boys drive
their parents up the wall. In his enthusiasm for animals,
Quentin Roosevelt took to spending all his leisure time in
a Washington pet shop. In fact, he was there so often that
his parents always knew where to look for him when he
turned up missing. A simple phone call to the proprietor,
and Quent would be pointed toward the door and sent
home.

The owner was not averse to the boy's company, since
Quentin often made himself useful helping to feed and
care for the various creatures in the multitude of cages.
After all no business is harmed when one of its steady cus-
tomers is a son of the President of the United States.

Unfortunately like any youngster, Quentin sometimes
abused his privileged status. The store's proprietor lived
in a small flat over the shop. One morning about five
o'clock, he was awakened by the tinkling of his bell. Outside, a blizzard raged. Raising the window and peering
down into the pre-dawn darkness, he saw the President's
son standing in snow up to his knees. "What do you
want?" demanded the irate shopowner. "How did you get
here anyway? Do you know what time it is?"

"Yes, I know, but I sneaked out," confessed Quentin

sheepishly. "The doorman didn't see me, he was dozing. Come on downstairs, let's feed the canaries."

The boy's adventure with the snakes took place when Quentin was thirteen years old. He was just returning from a vacation and the President sent his limousine to get him. But first, Quentin had to stop at the pet shop to see if anything had been added during his absence. To his great delight, there was something new: a cage or two of assorted snakes. Through some fast talking, coaxing, and wheedling, Quentin was allowed to take home four snakes on approval to show his father. He chose a five-foot King Snake, which he wrapped around his arm, and into a sack he dumped a Black Snake, a Gold-Banded Snake, and a Common Grass Snake. Quentin arrived at the White House and went looking for his father, who was in the west wing Oval Office holding an important political conference with several senators and party leaders. The boy barged in and hugged his father as the visitors watched tolerantly. Then Quentin dropped the snakes on the table.

Chaos and confusion resulted. Not only did the conference end then and there with legislators and party officials jumping out of chairs, scrambling around the table, and dashing from the room, but the snakes began a small war of their own. The King Snake attacked the Grass Snake while the Gold-Banded Snake and the Black Snake were off to a battle. Father and son had their hands full, tracking down, re-capturing, and re-bagging the slithering reptiles. Eventually this was accomplished and the snakes were returned to the pet shop forthwith.

Long experience with the President and his family should have taught the politicians that pets had the run of the White House, lying on chairs, sleeping under the tables, wandering about the corridors, or hiding in closets. Wherever a Roosevelt child was there was bound to be some kind of creature in the immediate vicinity. It could as easily have been a flying squirrel or a kangaroo rat carried conveniently in a pocket. At dinner, at breakfast, or at school, it was not unusual to see a small curious face emerge from a youngster's pocket and peer interestedly at the surroundings.

The Roosevelts acquired their pets in several ways. Some were gifts, some were stray pickups—one was practically thrown at the President!

As Mr. Roosevelt went whistle-stopping through Kansas, a little girl pushed a live badger onto the platform of the Presidential car. He took the animal home and presented it to the children as a new pet; they named him Josiah. The badger took his place among the other animals, playing with the youngsters, nipping their feet, and gorging on his favorite dish, milk and potatoes.

Alice Roosevelt, the eldest child, soon outgrew the garden variety of pets. As a vivacious young girl, she tore off on a trip to the Orient, and after being fêted in Japan and China, returned with an imposing array of fine presents.

23

Among them was Manchu, a spaniel given to her by the Empress of China.

Visiting the Roosevelts at the summer White House at Oyster Bay, Long Island, was like a trip to the zoo. There, one could encounter almost every imaginable beast: a lion, hyena, wildcat, coyote, five bears, two big parrots, an eagle, a barn owl, a zebra, plus a varied assortment of snakes, lizards, rabbits, rats, guinea pigs, dogs, cats, chipmunks, and canaries. Some of them were gifts of various rulers who knew the Roosevelts' passion for collecting animals. When a pet belonging to a large species grew too big for Oyster Bay or White House caretakers, they were usually donated to zoos.

A Roosevelt pet that puzzled everyone who saw it was a one-legged rooster. How the unfortunate fowl lost its limb is not clear. The children sought to assist it by devising an artificial leg, but nothing seemed to work. It didn't matter much because the rooster managed quite well by hopping around on the one leg.

There were some animals, creatures that normally could qualify as "Roosevelt-type" pets, which had to be killed. This was done in order to save the lives of other animals. Once, for example, Quentin came dashing in to tell his father that the raccoon was in the hickory grove. The President grabbed a rifle and was off on a chase. There was a valid reason for this hunt: The grove was not far from the place where the Roosevelt chickens were kept. Previously Roosevelt had spared the life of a possum wan-

dering about in that same area, and the possum had repaid the kindness by wreaking havoc in the coops. The
raccoon had done some damage, too. Once a wild animal
knows where natural food can be found, he will invariably
return again and again for a meal. The raccoon simply
had to go. Chasing away would do no good, for the beast
would only return. The local zoos had raccoons aplenty.
Thus there was no other way out. Soon Quentin and the
President returned carrying the dead animal by its hind
legs.

But such an incident was a great exception. President
Roosevelt loved animals, all animals, wild or tame, pedigreed or cur, stray tomcat or a pampered kitten. Perhaps,
like the scent of fear, there is also the scent of love, for
the creatures who saw the President reciprocated in kind.
Once when Theodore went to the theater, a dog mean-
dered onto the stage, stretched, and settled down to ob-
serve the activity. The audience thought this was hilarious,
and so did the President. He called out to the dog which
pricked up its ears at the sound of his voice, and with
one leap, the animal bounded into the Roosevelt box
and nestled in its occupant's lap. The play was forgotten
as every neck was craned in his direction. Finally in order
to allow the performance to continue, Roosevelt put the
dog back on the stage. Perhaps the audience had expected
the President to take the dog home. No doubt the reason
he didn't was the simple fact that the White House was
already filled to capacity with dogs. And no wonder!

For example, when Quentin's black-and-tan was lost and couldn't be found after a search of the entire city, the youngster brought home a similar one that was reported in the local dog pound.

Among other Roosevelt dogs was Pete, a bull terrier who bit the trousers of French Ambassador Jusseraud, then took a nip at the leg of a naval officer. Pete fancied himself cock of the walk for a while, until one day a strange dog inadvertently wandered into the grounds. With a low growl, Pete attacked. He promptly received a sound thrashing that cooled his ego for several days.

Sailor Boy, a Chesapeake retriever, liked to go boating with the children. If they refused to take him, or forgot he was there, he would jump into the water, swim out to the boat, and leap in anyway. Most dogs are terrified of sudden loud noises, but Sailor Boy liked to hear firecrackers exploding.

Jack, a terrier belonging to Kermit, was constantly bedeviled by a cat named Tom Quartz. He couldn't seem to avoid the cat no matter where he hid. Somehow Tom Quartz would ferret him out and jump on the poor dog's back.

And then there was Skip. President Roosevelt met Skip while on a bear hunt. He was just a small black mongrel, useless as a hunting dog, but no cuter, more engaging rascal ever sniffed the clear mountain air. At the beginning of a day's hunting, Skip would race off with the rest of the pack, doing his best to keep up. The heart and desire were there, but size and strength were lacking. Soon Skip would begin to tire and cast a beseeching look in the President's direction. Roosevelt would rein in his horse, reach down, pick up the dog, and seat him firmly on the saddle. When day was done, Skip slept at the foot of Roosevelt's bed, and snarled viciously at anyone who dared to approach. After the hunt, Skip had a new home, the White House.

Skip never lost his fondness for horseback riding. One of the most popular pets at the White House was a small Icelandic calico pony named Algonquin, and he and Skip became fast friends. Together they did a trick that the President and his children found delightful. The pony would go cantering about the lawn, suddenly Skip would race up, leap high, and land on Algonquin's back. The pony would snort, shake its head, swish its tail, and paw the ground in an unsuccessful effort to dislodge the dog. But everyone knew that Algonquin was only pretending to be annoyed, otherwise why would he slow his canter whenever he saw Skip come racing toward him?

Another Algonquin trick was the game of push. When the children had visitors, the pony would sneak up behind some youngster and begin to nudge him across the lawn.

Algonquin was the personal property of Archie Roosevelt. The pony was the one pet he loved more than any of the others, and he would often ride the pony to school, accompanied by a White House aide on a bicycle. When Archie had the measles and was confined to his bedroom,

Quentin contrived a visit from the pony. He sneaked Algonquin into the ground floor and onto the elevator, and then up the two flights to the bedroom.

There were, of course, many other horses for the Roosevelt family; all were avid horsemen. The former Rough Rider was an excellent equestrian, and almost nothing could deter him from an afternoon's ride; he even went out in the rain wearing a long rubber cape. His favorite was Bleistein, a great horse that could jump a hurdle five and a half feet high carrying the 185-pound President on his back.

In 1903 the elegant magazine *Town and Country* reported the President's leisurely rides in an article entitled "The President's Horses."

"At half past three o'clock Sergeant Mark P. Wilson of Troop K, 11th Cavalry who has been assigned as orderly to the President appears at the South Front of the White House, a private entrance, mounted on his own horse and leading Bleistein. He dismounts and walks the animals up and down until ten minutes before four. At that moment the President runs briskly down the steps and jumps into the saddle. Sometimes the President trots the horse out of the gate, but generally he walks him past the admiring crowd gathered there and lifts his hat with measured dignity. His orderly rides about 15 paces directly behind him and always carries a loaded revolver at his side. That is the program when the President rides alone. As he goes out into the suburbs he takes the loneliest roads he can find to get away from the turmoil of the city for a brief span. It is well that he is attended for in the event of an accident there could be otherwise no one to bring in the tidings. But the President is often accompanied by Mrs. Roosevelt and sometimes by friends."

Although Bleistein's tail was docked, Roosevelt considered that a needless cruelty and managed to get a bill into the Senate forbidding the docking of horses' tails in Washington, D.C. It never became a law. Considering the number of pets wandering through the lives of the Roosevelts, the problem of naming them all sometimes got out of hand. Other horse names ranged from the usual—Renown, Rusty, Jocko, Gray Dawn, to the more imaginative—Root, Wyoming, and Yagenka. The carriage horses were simply General and Judge. Sometimes the youngsters used the names of real people, probably friends of the family. Eli was the name given to Teddy Roosevelt, Jr.'s brightly colored macaw. This was a peculiar bird whose speaking voice could be heard half way through the rooms of the White House. Bill was a horned toad who lived on the South Portico for a number of years. Jonathan was a piebald rat who liked to climb on anything that happened to be handy, be it furniture or human. Another Jonathan was a grouchy, short-tempered black bear (which later became the property of the Washington Zoo), dubbed Jonathan Edwards in honor of the famous cleric and ancestor of Mrs. Roosevelt.

Then there was a clutch of guinea pigs owned by

Kermit Roosevelt. Two were named Dewey Senior and Dewey Junior, for Admiral Dewey. Others were named Bob Evans, Bishop Doan (of Albany, New York), and Father O'Grady, the latter being the name of the neighborhood priest. Sometimes these names resulted in startling situations. Once when the President was entertaining an important dignitary, the children rushed in shouting, "Poppa, Poppa, Father O'Grady just had children!"

Sometimes the President's consideration of animals sprang from his sense of humor. Slippers was a great cat with six toes. It would wander off frequently and be gone for days and weeks at a time, but it had a sixth sense as far as social goings-on were concerned. The White House employees always noticed that it managed to get back just before a big diplomatic dinner was to be held. The dignified cat wasn't the least bit fazed by the distinguished guests from across the Atlantic. It showed up one night when President Roosevelt was leading his guests from the East Room down the corridor to the State Dining Room. The President was walking with the wife of a guest of honor, an important ambassador. Close behind followed a line of noted guests, ambassadors, ministers, and other officials, all according to their rank in the diplomatic world. Suddenly the procession slowed down. There on the rug lay Slippers, right in the path of everybody, stretched full length, blinking lazily. The President had seen Slippers, but if he stopped to pick him up, he realized that it would hold back the entire line, so he gave an amused bow to the ambassador's wife and escorted her around the cat. Every important guest followed with a lady on his arm doing the same thing. Thus the whole diplomatic corps gave way to Slippers.

It has been said of President Theodore Roosevelt that he knew how to handle all boys and all animals. That is true. He taught his sons how to box and shoot, how to ride, swim, and sail a boat. To him such skills symbolized manliness, a clean mind, and a clean body. He taught them reverence for all forms of life. Perhaps the following story best illustrates the values he tried to instill in his children and how well he succeeded:

The President sent his children to Washington public schools. A reporter asked the boys how it felt to go to school with "ordinary" boys. Without hesitation one of the Roosevelt sons—it could have been any of them—replied, "My father says there are only tall boys and short boys, good boys and bad boys. That's all the kinds of boys there are."

Chapter 3

GEORGE WASHINGTON'S HORSES
AND HOUNDS

M OUNT VERNON is a wonderful playground for children.
It was a beautiful drive out from Washington in my
day. I used to jump up and down when a visitor from
Missouri had to be entertained. I always suggested Mount
Vernon. Mother didn't share my enthusiastic sightseeing
proclivities, but I used any excuse to see Mount Vernon,
or the Robert E. Lee mansion at Arlington, and pretend
I was a visitor in the times of Washington or Lee.

A child's imagination is boundless, and I had no difficulty seeing myself as a bewigged eighteenth-century lady
in a hoop skirt surrounded, of course, by handsome, bewigged eighteenth-century gentlemen in laces and knee
breeches.

If it is true that a man is known by the life he leads—
and the animals he surrounds himself with—then Squire
Washington was as much a patrician and aristocrat as any

mannered English duke or earl across the ocean. Like them, it was his pleasure to ride to hounds. As a youth of twenty, living at Mount Vernon, which he had inherited from his wealthy half-brother Lawrence, he cut a dashing figure on horseback, racing after the baying hounds.

It might be added that it was the grey fox that was most often seen in those early years. The red fox began to infiltrate the Virginia region from the eastern shore during the winter of 1779 and 1780 when a hard freeze enabled them to cross the ice-covered portions of Chesapeake Bay.

The fox hunts continued throughout most of Washington's adult life. The beginning of a typical hunt day might see him breakfasting by candlelight on corn cakes and milk; at daybreak he and his guests would ride out looking for a fox. In the role of huntsman was Billy Lee, the valet who followed General Washington through the Revolution. Billy would have the horn on his back as he rode mounted on a horse named Chinkling. Then the whole group would tear across the rolling hills of Fairfax County. Wearing a blue coat, scarlet waistcoat, buckskin breeches, boots and velvet cap, carrying his whip, Washington was usually in the lead.

One hunt ended in such a peculiar way that Washington saw fit to enter it into his journal. On January 23, 1770, he wrote, "Went a-hunting after breakfast and found a fox at Muddy Hole and killed her (it being a Bitch) after a chase of better than two hours and after treeing her twice, the last of which time she fell dead out of the tree after being there several minutes, apparently well." (I suppose even foxes have heart attacks.)

As a rule the hunts ended in a manner that might have been recorded by any of the nineteenth-century English novelists. The ladies and gentlemen who participated in a day's outing gathered in one of the mansions, perhaps Mount Vernon or Belvoir or Gunston Hall, where a magnificent dinner would be served. Later the ladies would congregate on their own to gossip while the gentlemen discussed the day's hunt over glasses of Madeira.

The woman Washington married shared many of his interests, including horses. The former Martha Dandridge Custis was an excellent rider. On more than one occasion, horses figured prominently in her girlhood pranks. It is said that she rode her horse Fatima up and down the staircases of the mansion owned by her indulgent uncle, William Dandridge. When she and the squire of Mount Vernon were married, the ceremony was performed at the plantation she had inherited from her first husband. Oddly enough, the mansion had long been called the White House.

In order to chase the fox properly, Washington was required to keep stables of horses and kennels full of hounds. An honored place in the stables was given to the horse presented to him by General Braddock, with whom Washington had been a young officer serving with the British in the French and Indian War. Not all of his horses were used exclusively for the hunt. Washington also fancied himself a breeder. He was most capable in that respect.

During the early years of his marriage he kept a succession of stallions for his own mares and those of his neighbors. These included such stalwarts as Samson, Steady, Leonidas, and Traveller. The latter was also the name of Lee's horse in the Civil War. In addition, there was a magnificent full-blooded Arabian steed named Magnolia, probably the finest horse ever owned by Washington or any of his Virginia peers. He was inordinately fond of these stallions. They could be called pets in every sense of the word, and he took great care to see that they were properly attended to.

On those occasions when he was absent from his estates, Washington instructed his managers to advertise the stallions or exhibit them at fairs. When another breeder desired the services of a Washington stallion, the mare was brought to Mount Vernon or to any of his other pastures where the stud horses were kept. Foals were guaranteed. Sometimes Washington had difficulty collecting his fees.

Squire Washington was not above ministering to an injured horse personally. An entry in a diary dated February 22, 1760, his twenty-eighth birthday, reveals that one of his horses, Jolly, had his right foreleg "mashed to pieces." Washington wrote, "Did it up as well as I could." The next notation was Saturday, February 23, "Had the horse slung upon canvas, and his leg fresh set. Following

Markleham's directions as well as I could." Unfortunately his efforts were to no avail. Two days later the horse fell out of the sling and was so badly injured that it had to be destroyed.

Washington was continually stocking the estate. After he became President, Washington made a special trip to Lancaster, Pennsylvania, where he bought thirteen additional breeding mares, paying the then astronomical price of 317 pounds, 17 shillings, and sixpence for the lot. Considering that the average mare could have been had for the going price of 5 or 6 pounds each, the ones Washington selected must have been exceptional. By the end of 1785 he was stabling and pasturing some 130 horses at his farm holding.

Washington attached a great deal of sentimental value to two of the horses that served him well during the Revolution. One was Blueskin, a dark iron-grey stallion, with great endurance over a long run. To Washington, sound wind in a horse was of first importance. It was not merely the rigors of the hunt he was considering. During his service with Braddock, he had had two horses shot out from under him as he made his escape from enemy ambush. Before Braddock died near Fort Duquesne, he gave his favorite white horse to young Major Washington.

Washington's other favorite was a chestnut named Nelson. It was while mounted on Nelson that General Washington accepted the surrender of General Cornwallis at Yorktown. Nelson became as tame as a house pet, running with a whinny to the pasture fence when he heard Washington call his name. Both Blueskin and Nelson lived to a ripe old age.

As a horseman Washington had no equal among succeeding Presidents. Jefferson said of him, "Washington was the best horseman of his age, and the most magnificent figure that could be seen on horseback." Another friend of Washington's, de Chastellux, wrote of his host's tremendous skill with horses. "The weather being fair on the 26th, I got on horseback after breakfasting with the General. He was so attentive as to give me the horse he rode the day of my arrival which I greatly commended. I found him as good as he is handsome, but above all, perfectly well broke and well trained. He had a good mouth, easy in hand, and stopping short in a gallop without bearing the bit. I mention these minute particulars because it is the General himself who breaks all his own horses, and he is a very excellent and bold horseman, leaping the highest fences and going extremely quick without standing upon his stirrups, bearing on the bridle or letting his horse run wild, circumstances which young men look upon as so essential a part of English horsemanship that they would rather break a leg or an arm than renounce them."

From Washington's voluminous notes, it would appear that the year 1768 was an active one for hound-raising. Among his dogs were Mopsey, Taster, Cloe, Tipler, Forester, Captain, and Lady. An entry in his journal dated

August 6, 1768, reveals that Lady had four puppies which were named Rover, Vulcan, Sweetlips, and Searcher. Washington was constantly trying to raise his dogs according to scientific principles. He strove to get pure strains out of his breeds, but dogs will be dogs, and sometimes their mating was not according to Washington's desires. They were also plagued with illnesses. On one occasion he notes that he was forced to anoint all the hounds having the mange "with Hogs Lard and Brimstone."

After the Revolution ended, there was a period of six years before Washington assumed the Presidency. He spent all that time in Mount Vernon devoting himself fully to his farms and animals. His former comrade at arms, Lafayette, knowing how the General admired good dogs, sent him a pack of French hounds, consisting of two males and three females. They soon became his favorites. These were massive dogs—vicious, snarling beasts, so fierce that a huntsman had to oversee their feeding lest they tear each other to shreds in their lunges to get at the food. Washington thought this the perfect temperament for hunting dogs. He delighted in visiting their kennel every morning and evening.

The biggest of these animals was Vulcan, not to be confused with an earlier dog of the same name. He was so large that it was possible for a small boy to ride on his back, as if Vulcan were a pony. This hound was a fast, wily creature, always hungry. If there was food anywhere in the vicinity, Vulcan would be sure to find it. Mrs.

Washington discovered this trait in Vulcan to her dismay after she had personally supervised the cooking of an immense dinner ham. Somehow Vulcan got into the kitchen, seized the meat with his great jaws, and dashed through the whole staff like a zigzagging football player carrying the ball. He went straight to his kennel where he proceeded to devour it at his leisure. It is reported that the General roared with glee when informed of the incident.

At various times in his life Washington also tried raising other kinds of stock, but these could not be called pets. Yet he was interested in them. Very few farmers in Virginia tried sheep raising, but as early as 1758, Washington had begun experimenting with such flocks. His overseer in that year reported 65 sheep and 48 lambs. Seven years later the total number was raised to 156. In his efforts to improve the strain of sheep, he bought a special young English ram that he bred with 65 ewes.

Washington also tried raising deer, turkeys, geese, and mules. The deer were kept in one section of his estate, but were continually getting out. Soon deer overran the estate but a number of them stayed in the wooded section where they were born and raised. They seemed to know it was safest there—Washington was troubled quite often by poachers.

During Washington's Presidency his horses became the most petted, polished, pampered beasts in the land. No White House pets in the future would ever receive the care and attention given these horses. When George Washington took office, New York City was the nation's capital. The President's palace, as it was called, was a fine brick house located at number 10 Cherry Street, a short distance from Franklin Square.

Stable boys began to curry and groom the horses promptly at sunrise. The master of the stables, Bishop by name, was a martinet of the first order. He would stalk through the stables, muslin handkerchief in hand, and stop beside some horse that he thought looked not quite up to par. He would rub the handkerchief over the horse's hide, and woe betide the stableboy if the muslin showed a stain. The luckless fellow was punished on the spot!

One Presidential globe-shaped carriage was cream-colored, with panels painted to represent the four seasons, and was drawn by six bay horses. It must have been quite a show.

When the capital was shifted to Philadelphia, Washington's new official home was the Robert Morris mansion located on High Street. There the horses, if possible, were given more meticulous care than ever.

The stables were headed by a man named Gentleman John who saw his chores as a matter of life and death. The night before the horses were to be ridden, they were entirely covered with a paste that contained whiting ingredients. The steeds were bedded down for the night on clean straw, and covered over with layers of clean cloth. In the morning when the paste was hardened, it was rubbed in, burnished, and polished until every coat gleamed with a glossy, satin finish. Their hoofs were blackened and polished, and as a final touch their mouths were washed and their teeth picked clean.

There were a dozen horses in the Presidential stable during the Philadelphia residence, ten fine bays and two chargers.

Washington's wife and children had the usual run of dogs and other pets, but they did not particularly interest him. Mrs. Washington had a parrot to which she was devoted; she had always been fond of birds. Before she married for the first time a previous suitor had tamed a mockingbird and presented it to her.

Washington's lively step-daughter Nellie Custis must have found the fine stables irresistible, as well as the other pets. She wrote a friend in a zany letter: "I have learned to ride on horseback and am very delighted with it, believe me ... I have spent ten days most agreeably teaching our pretty green pet [the parrot] to sing 'Pauvre Madelon' ... I forgot to tell you the name of my nag. It is Rozinante." And she signed it—"Myself, harum-scarum sans souci."

At the end of his administration, Mr. Washington moved back to his Virginia estate. On the final moving day he was like any other husband, complaining that all the details were left to him. The packing and shipping were almost more than he could bear. Trunks and furniture were piled high on the wagon with his wife's parrot cage perched atop everything. Harassed, he wrote a note to his secretary, Tobias Lear: "On one side I am called upon to remember the parrot, and on the other to remember the dog. For my own part, I should not pine much if both were forgot."

Washington's last years spent on his estate were years of splendor, honor, and dignity. His passion for horses never left him. He bought two horses of the type then known as Narragansetts. They were distinguished by their peculiar running style, moving both legs on the same side at the same time. Today they're called pacers. One of them caused Washington's only recorded fall from a horse.

He was returning from Alexandria, Virginia, with a few companions, when he stopped at a roadside fire to warm himself. When he tried to remount, the horses started before the General could be seated, and Washington slipped to the ground. He was unhurt and his horse soon recaptured.

On a raw, blustery day in December, 1799, when he was sixty-seven years old, Washington went for a ride. He returned chilled to the bone. A respiratory complication set in, and in two days he was dead.

Undoubtedly it was a combination of factors that led to our first President's interest in horses. All the landed gentry of the time devoted themselves to the hunt and prided themselves on their stables. Washington did the same. Also he knew the military value of a good horse, as did several future generals who became President. But the generals had one or two favorites and never assembled as large and complex a series of stables as did Washington. In that respect the Father of our Country was unique among Chief Executives.

Chapter 4

LADDIE BOY AND MR. HARDING

When World War I ended the Republicans campaigned with the phrase, "Back to Normalcy with Harding." They were reflecting America's desire for peace. Certainly short flapper skirts, bootlegging, and speakeasies were not part of our normal pattern of life. But the "normalcy" catch phrase referred to the more peaceful ways of routine local issues, as opposed to the less familiar international problems. America was still predominantly a rural nation, and most voters were ready to turn away from the affairs of state in Paris, London, and Berlin.

In this mood there was nothing more peaceful, more idyllic, than the story of a man and his dog. It helps if the man is a farmboy-made-good, and if the dog is of a type familiar to most people. Warren Gamaliel Harding was born on a farm, and Airedales were quite common in America, although Laddie Boy was surely an uncommon dog.

This was a match that must have been made in political

heaven. The President and his dog understood each other very well, but for that matter Mr. Harding seemed devoted to the welfare of all human and animal life. He never referred to any beast as a dumb animal, simply because he felt they were not dumb, but had their own means of communication that humans failed to grasp.

That Mr. Harding took all animals seriously was a matter of record before he entered the White House. In private conversation with friends, he said that humans were infinitely more cruel, more "inhuman," than dogs. As editor of the *Marion Star,* in Marion, Ohio, he never hesitated to put those sentiments in print. An editorial he wrote concerning the poisoning of a neighbor's dog by an unknown person is poignant and perceptive.

"He was Edgewood Hub in the register, a mark of his breeding, but to us just Hub, a little Boston terrier whose sentient eyes mirrored the fidelity and devotion of his loyal heart. The veterinary said he was poisoned; perhaps he was; his mute suffering suggested it.

"One is reluctant to believe that a human being who claims man's estate could be so hateful a coward, as ruthless to torture and kill a trusting victim, made defenseless through his confidence in human masters, but there are such. . . .

"Perhaps you wouldn't devote these lines to a dog, but Hub was a *Star* office visitor nearly every day of the six years in which he deepened attachments. He was a grateful and devoted dog with a dozen lovable attributes, and

45

it somehow voices the yearnings of a broken companionship to pay his memory deserved tribute. . . .

"Hub was loving and loyal with a jealousy that attests its equality. He was reserved, patient, faithful. He was sympathetic, more than humanly so, for no lure could be devised to call him from the sickbed of mistress or master. . . .

"He couldn't speak our language although he somehow understood, and was eloquent with uttering eye and wagging tail, and other expressions of knowing dogs. . . . Whether the Creator planned it so, or environment and human companionship have made it so, men may learn richly through the love and fidelity of a brave and devoted dog."

From that editorial it is obvious that Mr. Harding bestowed a great deal of affection on dogs. He had many dogs before he went to the White House, and several of them moved to Washington with him. It seemed fitting that the first gift he received as President of the United States would be a small, shaggy, somewhat homely Airedale puppy, named Caswell Laddie Boy, presented by an old friend, Mr. Marshall Sheppey of Toledo, Ohio.

As a rule President Harding had no special favorites among his dogs. To him they were unique individuals, each with its own personality traits. But when this precocious pup appeared on the scene, Mr. Harding found himself completely helpless before the bright eyes, cocked head, the alert, intelligent face.

In a short time, Laddie Boy was the undisputed Presidential pet, making his presence known and felt in the White House. A dog's life in Laddie Boy's case was that of an affluent human. The Airedale had his own valet, a man named Willy Jackson, whose job it was to care for the pup's needs and wants. Laddie Boy was given daily baths, fed a bowl of broth and dog biscuits, and, of course, managed to cadge choice bits of the President's breakfast and lunch as well.

Laddie Boy sat in on important Presidential meetings. The term "sat in" is used advisedly, for he was provided with his own special chair at Cabinet meetings. Laddie Boy received numerous invitations to attend special functions and affairs, some of which were graciously accepted. On May 11, 1921, the Humane Education Society held a "Be Kind to Animals" parade. Leading the procession was Laddie Boy, seated atop his own float imparting the proper air of dignity as demanded by the occasion.

Laddie Boy became one of dogdom's great figures, famous nationally and internationally. On Sunday, July 17, 1921, the editorial section of the *Washington Star* printed a mock interview with Laddie Boy that ran on for nearly an entire page, including two editorial cartoons. The Airedale commented on the sheep kept by Mr. Woodrow Wilson; lashed out against a ban on Mexican hairless dogs, and chastised the Attorney General about mail sled dogs in Alaska. He suggested that Henry A. Wallace investigate dog biscuits. (This Wallace was the father of

Franklin D. Roosevelt's Vice President.) Laddie Boy advocated an eight-hour day for all watch dogs, talked about Prohibition, and gave his opinion of such people as Thomas Edison, Albert Einstein, and the entire Harding Cabinet. The interview was conducted with great tongue-in-cheek seriousness, and the responses were delivered in the same manner.

Mr. Harding, like some other Presidents, was fond of golf. Laddie Boy retrieved lost balls. Several aides remarked that Laddie Boy seemed to smile at the good drives and howl at the slices and hooks. In the *Star* interview, Laddie Boy denied that story emphatically, saying that he never howled because it would be undignified, and that he had only retrieved one ball from the rough.

As Laddie Boy's fame spread, he was deluged with sacksful of letters and many gifts. Some of the letters were from dog owners who claimed that their pets were related to the Harding Airedale, that he was father or brother to the dogs they owned. For the most part these claims were without foundation. Actually Laddie Boy was the son of Champion Tintern Tip Top, and a half-brother, Laddie Buck, moved into the White House with the Coolidges. Gifts to Laddie Boy were the usual variety of toy bones, rubber balls, sweaters, blankets, and other paraphernalia peculiar to dogs. The one gift that caused a stir was the birthday present sent by Laddie Boy's father. It was a huge four-tiered cake made up of dog biscuits and covered with white icing. Naturally such a magnificent cake called

48

for an appropriate party which was duly held. Attending were Laddie Boy's companions, the other dogs quartered in the White House stables, plus a number belonging to Washington friends and neighbors. Like any other social event of significance the affair was covered by reporters and photographers.

Laddie Boy was not the only dog President Harding received as a gift. Another that struck his fancy was the handsome, pure white English bulldog named Oh Boy. At first the President quartered the newcomer in the stables; he wanted to keep the bulldog away from the Airedale, fearful that the two might clash. Mr. Harding needn't have worried. Laddie Boy was top dog and somehow he always made sure that everyone knew it, including the other dogs. After all, he was the proud possessor of Washington dog license Number One, and the personal friend of the President, accompanying him on walks around the White House grounds.

After the first few tentative approaches, Laddie Boy and Oh Boy became fast friends, and were soon romping together along the halls and in the rooms of the White House. Oh Boy was probably aware that he could never displace Laddie Boy in the affections of their master.

The President's newspapers continued to be delivered personally by Laddie Boy, and Oh Boy was given a place of honor at Laddie Boy's birthday party. Laddie Boy proved to be a decided asset to the President's social planning. Once the House of Representatives held a seemingly endless debate about the advisability of doing away with the United States Marine Band which furnished the music for the President and his guests at social functions. Some tax-cutting congressmen said that Mr. Harding should provide his own music and save the people's money. Others insisted that the Marine Band music was an established tradition.

Representative James Henry MacLafferty (Republican of California) finally put an end to the tedious talk. He bluntly asked his colleagues which they preferred, "The President keeping his Marine Band music or listening to Laddie Boy racing around the White House grounds, howling, with a tomato can tied to his tail?" The Marine Band remained intact, but the idea of tying a can to Laddy Boy's tail would never have occurred to Mr. Harding.

Mr. Harding was probably the only Chief Executive on record who saved a dog's life by a form of executive clemency. While thumbing through his newspapers, the President came upon an item concerning a condemned dog. The unfortunate animal, nondescript, of no particular breed, was sentenced to death by a Pennsylvania Justice of the Peace because its owner, an alien, had probably brought him into the country illegally. Mr. Harding wrote to Governor William Cameron Sproul, saying how touched he and Mrs. Harding were by the dog's predicament. He wrote the letter as a personal appeal, realizing that the Justice could hardly refuse such a plea from the President. Governor Sproul issued an order pardoning the dog.

President Harding used another letter to comment on the Tea Pot Dome and Veterans Administration scandals involving the Secretary of the Interior and the Attorney General. Ostensibly Laddie Boy received a letter from a dog named Tiger, who performed in vaudeville. Tiger's letter, commending Laddie Boy's loyalty to his master, was printed in an issue of the *National* magazine. In answering the note, Mr. Harding pointed out that man and dog alike could be undone by bad associations, by trusting the wrong people who use friendship to gain their own personal ends.

Although Laddie Boy took several trips with his master, there were many times when taking him on extended journeys was impractical. The Airedale became accustomed to the frequent absences of his master, and never lost his patience while awaiting his return. Laddie Boy would look in on the canaries, belonging to Mrs. Harding, and the pen of turkeys that the President had received from friends in Texas, Tennessee, and Kentucky. Mostly, Laddie Boy would sit quietly, springing to the alert whenever a motor car turned through the gates. In his mind, an automobile had taken his master and mistress away so he felt sure that the same kind of conveyance would bring them back.

In July, 1923, President Harding began a tour of the western states and Alaska. On the return trip, he was taken ill at Grant's Pass, Oregon, and rushed to a hos-

51

pital in San Francisco. He died there on August 2. Laddie Boy was at the White House waiting expectantly when the funeral motorcade arrived back in Washington bearing the body of his master. He leaped up, but there was no reply to his joyous welcoming yelps. It was said later that White House attachés shook their heads sadly and wondered how they were going to make the dog understand what had happened.

On August 3, 1923, the Associated Press carried the following news item: "There was one member of the White House household today who couldn't quite comprehend the air of sadness which overhung the executive mansion. It was Laddie Boy, President Harding's Airedale friend and companion. Coming to the White House a rawboned, callow pup, Laddie Boy has, in two years, grown to the estate of dignity and wholesome respect for his official surroundings."

Mrs. Harding could not bear the thought of keeping the dog. In her memory, Laddie Boy and her husband were too intertwined. She later gave Laddie Boy to Harry Barker, a Secret Service man who had protected the President on many of his trips.

Mr. Louis Newman of the Newsboys' Associations began a movement to have a statuette made of Laddie Boy which could be presented to Mrs. Harding as their tribute to the late President. Every newsboy in the country was asked to contribute one penny of his earnings. After all, Mr. Harding had been a newspaper man himself and it

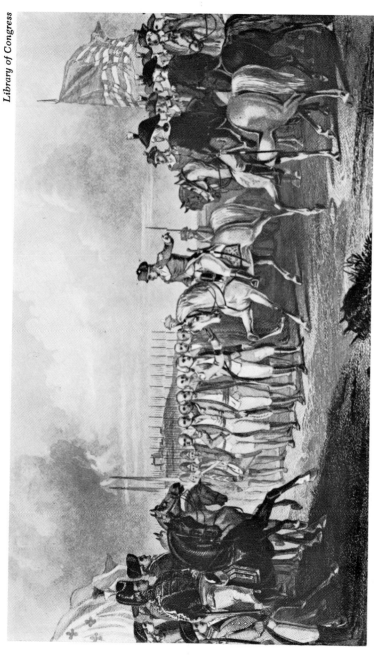

1. Washington's most famous warhorse, Nelson, witnessed the surrender of Cornwallis at Yorktown, 1781.

2. Andrew Jackson, the "race-horse" President, had numerous mounts. He is here shown on Sam Patches. His favorite was the famous Truxton.

3. When Gen. Zachary Taylor moved to the White House, Old Whitey was pastured on the lawn, where visitors pulled hair from his tail.

THE STABLE OF THE WHITE HOUSE.—[Photographed by L. E. Walker.]

4. General Grant's White House stable, built in 1864, was rigidly managed by Albert, who talked and ate with the animals.

5. The last White House stable, built by Theodore Roosevelt, housed his Bleistein, Archie's Algonquin, and later, Taft's cow Pauline.

6. Newly elected President Nixon was presented with champion King Timahoe, a gorgeous Irish setter, given to him by his staff.

Washington Post

7. The glare of publicity spotlighted Julie Nixon's poodle Vicky and Tricia's Welsh terrier Pasha on the day they moved in.

UPI

8. Weimaraners were fashionable, but the White House proved too frenetic for the nerves of Heidi, the pet of President Eisenhower.

9. My own dog Mike, an Irish setter, who always acted like a puppy, was moved out to save his digestion from tidbits offered by the staff.

10. Neither my father nor I remember this little character, who arrived in December, 1947. He made a one-day news item.

11. No incident ever caused more of a ruckus than this one—LBJ pulling Him by the ears. The next day, a national furor arose.

12. At first sight, President Johnson fell in love with mutt Yuki, found abandoned at a gas station in Texas by Luci and her husband.

13. Another international incident rose over Khrushchev's gift to Caroline Kennedy of Pushinka, mother of Charley's pups.

14. Jacqueline Kennedy and John-John are riding Sardar, a gift of Ayub Khan of Pakistan, and Caroline is on Macaroni.

15. Even at four years of age, Caroline Kennedy was expected to care for her two ponies, Tex, a gift of Vice President Johnson,

and Macaroni. Here she dismounts, unsaddles, waters, and leads
her pets to their stalls in the stables.

16. The Kennedy collection visits the Kennedy compound at Hyannis-port, Massachusetts—Clipper, Charley, the pups, Shannon, and Wolf.

17. The enchanting Caroline always stole the limelight, except when Shannon, or one of the many other Kennedy pets, shared it with her.

18. Kennedy pets always went on trips with the First Family—Clipper here boards the Kennedy yacht *Honey Fitz* for a cruise.

19. Tourists and Washingtonians were always feeding White House animals through the fence—and

was simply a matter of remembering one of their own. Circulation managers forwarded the money as it came in. A well-known sculptor, Miss Bashka Paeff, agreed to do the statuette. Laddie Boy posed for no less than fifteen sittings.

Unfortunately, Mrs. Harding died before the statuette could be presented to her. It was turned over to the Smithsonian Institution. Millions of dog lovers have seen and admired it. To those who understand such devotion, it simply represents a dog whose master just happened to be the President of the United States.

Chapter 5

THE LINCOLN PETS

ONE of the few pets Abraham Lincoln had during his childhood was a pig. Those who work with pigs maintain that they are extremely intelligent. Lincoln's boyhood pig must have been one of the smartest ever, for the youngster taught it to play hide and seek. When the pig grew to full size, it turned out to be a big one, and Abe rode on its back as though it were a pony.

Perhaps because he remembered this pet so well, years later Mr. Lincoln played the role of a rescuer to a pig. One of the tales told most often about him has to do with a pig that was stuck in the mud by the side of the road. Young lawyer Lincoln was riding by, saw the pig's plight, waded into the mud, and freed the screaming animal, setting it on firmer ground. The pig departed without a backward glance, leaving a muck-spattered Lincoln to endure the jibes of his traveling companions.

Aside from the horse he needed for transportation, there

is no record of any special Lincoln pet during his bachelor days nor immediately after he married Mary Todd. It was said that she did not want any animals in her house.

However, when the children came, Mrs. Lincoln did not deny them at least an occasional pet.

In Springfield, the family usually kept cats, and Mrs. Lincoln referred to them as her husband's "hobby." He would often sit down on the floor and talk to one or another of them and play gently with them.

Another pet was a medium-sized, yellow-brown mongrel pup named Fido. To be accurate, only half of Fido belonged to Willy and Tad Lincoln. The other half belonged to the Roll family who lived down the block. The Lincoln and the Roll boys were long-time friends, and they reached an agreement whereby they shared the dog. Fido heartily approved of this arrangement because by moving back and forth between the two houses he sometimes managed to get two dinners. The pup must have had a winning personality, because Mrs. Lincoln allowed him to curl up on the boys' beds.

Abraham Lincoln often enjoyed a frolic on the floor with the boys and Fido, and Lincoln buffs insist that it was Fido who inspired one of his favorite parables. While rolling on the floor during an evening romp with the dogs and his sons, Mr. Lincoln suddenly asked,

"If you were to call a tail a leg, how many legs would this dog have?" Five was the answer the boys gave.

"No," replied Lincoln, "calling a tail a leg doesn't make it a leg."

Why Fido did not accompany the Lincolns to the White House has never been fully explained. One version has it that the railroad did not allow dogs aboard trains in those days. But surely this rule would have been suspended for a President-elect. It is also possible that Mr. Lincoln believed that a half-ownership did not entitle Willy and Tad to take the dog permanently. For whatever reason, Fido was left behind to get along as best he could with one set of masters.

Lincoln in Washington received a report late in 1863 from his former barber, William Florville:

"Tell Taddy that his (and Willys) Dog is a live and Kicking doing well he stays mostly at John E. Rolls with his Boys who are about the size now that Tad and Willy were when they left for Washington."

Tad and Willy were promised a couple of ponies when they were settled at the White House, and the President was as good as his word. Soon Tad and Willy—they were inseparable—were clopping through the streets of Washington with Mr. Lincoln astride his own horse trailing not far behind.

In addition to the ponies, Tad was presented with a dog and Willy was given a cat. These two animals created quite a stir among the White House staff, for on the same day the dog had pups and the cat had kittens. News of the multiple births was circulated through Congress, the Cabinet, and foreign legations. The one who leaked the information, and boasted about it, too—was Abraham Lincoln himself. He even had a hand in thinking up new names for the pups and kittens in both litters.

The death of little Willy only a year after he came to Washington was a crushing blow to the Lincolns. Tad especially felt the loss. He became listless, hollow-eyed; his pony remained in the stables, unridden and unpetted. As he explained his feelings, "The ponies make me miss Willy even more." Later Lincoln himself was deeply saddened when Willy's and Tad's ponies died in a stable fire in the winter of 1864. The President had rushed out in the night and tried unsuccessfully to rescue them, but it was too late.

The sight of Tad moping around the Executive Mansion was almost more than President Lincoln could bear. Before the tragedy, he had been a high-spirited, first-class mischief-maker. That was how he received his nickname. Tad had been christened Thomas, but he was such a fidgeter, so "wriggly," that Mr. Lincoln dubbed him Tadpole, later shortening it to Tad.

The President tried to restore his son to his usual mischievous self by giving him other pets, and people also sent Tad pets. From Philadelphia came a pair of pink-eyed white rabbits. Lincoln wrote to the sender:

Executive Mansion
April 2, 1862

Dear Sir

Allow me to thank you in behalf of my little son for the present of White Rabbits. He is very much pleased with them.

Yours truly,
Abraham Lincoln

Tad often stroked their soft, silky fur, but nothing aroused the gleam that shines in the eyes of a small boy when he receives a pet he really likes. Happily, that was solved by a pair of goats.

Modern city dwellers accustomed to dogs, cats, birds, and other small animals may not realize how popular goats were as pets a hundred years ago. They eat practically anything they can get close to, the female gives milk, and children can hitch them to small carts.

Mr. and Mrs. Lincoln and Tad went riding one day, and Tad saw some goats. For the first time in months the boy began to smile as he watched them chew up a few things.

Noting his son's interest, the President instructed an aide, Mr. William Tisdale, to scout around and come back with a pair of goats. Mr. Tisdale found a pretty good pair that he bought for five dollars each.

The President commented on the trouble they might cause Mr. Tisdale, and when the aide asked how, Mr.

58

Lincoln said that Tad wouldn't give him any peace till there was a harness for the goats. Tisdale was only too glad to get the saddler of the nearby cavalry company to make the proper gear.

The goats were immediately named Nanny and Nanko, and for the next few months, the White House was a happier bedlam of noise.

Tad had never owned a goat before, and with the typical inquisitive approach of a ten-year-old, he tried to find out just how much fun he could have with them. He tied a rope to their collars and pretended they were oversize dogs. That was a rather tame sport. Tad tried butting them in the head, but they butted back, so there was no point pursuing that.

He turned the goats loose and chased after them, whooping and yelling as he raced across the lawn. That wasn't such a good idea, for the goats got into the flower beds, causing Mr. Watt, the White House gardener, to turn purple with rage as he saw his prize iris being trampled under their hoofs. Mr. Watt, knowing how these animals chewed shrubs and flowers, never was a goat-admirer anyway.

In time the goats were broken to the harness and learned to pull a cart. Then Tad, with the children of aides and neighbors, would pile into the wagon and go shrieking around the grounds, barreling through flower beds, shrubs, and over freshly sown ground. It is said that

Mr. Watt was heard to mutter dark threats against Tad's goats.

On one occasion, the goats ran afoul of Mrs. Lincoln when they appeared inside the White House, and she never did quite forgive them. The first she knew of it was when they showed up in the kitchen looking for a handout. She had no idea how they got there in the first place, but before she had time to find out she was interrupted by the disconcerting hubbub of female voices. Then she found out what had happened.

It seems that Tad had decided to hold his own indoor track meet with the goats. He had harnessed them one behind the other and fastened both to the kitchen chair, which was his racing cart. The voices Mrs. Lincoln heard belonged to a group of Boston ladies who were visiting the White House and were then admiring the East Room. Suddenly Tad came tearing through in his goat-driven racing cart. To me the picture of a small boy riding a kitchen chair pulled by two goats through an official ladies' reception in the East Room is irresistible. Mrs. Lincoln considered accusing her husband of putting the whole idea in Tad's head, especially when she found him in the kitchen laughing so hard that even a handkerchief clapped over his mouth failed to muffle the sounds. The team of Nanny and Nanko was disbanded while Tad was accompanying his mother on a trip to Vermont. The boy had extracted a promise that his father would see to it that the goats were cared for and would issue periodic reports on their welfare. The President received a letter from Mary asking that money be sent to her and ending: "Tad says are the goats well?"

Lincoln answered sending the money and concluding: "Tell Tad the goats and father are very well—especially the goats."

Mr. Lincoln tried his best to look after the goats and the Civil War at the same time, but the two tasks were more than any President could handle. That was more the goats' fault than his.

Nanko was the better behaved of the pair, although both were frisky, but at least Nanko stayed put in the stables, while Nanny kept getting out and making a bee-line for the flowers.

Finally, to keep Mr. Watts from having apoplexy, the President had Nanny brought into the White House. Nanny wandered forlornly through the corridors, got on Tad's bed and curled up, contentedly chewing her cud. Mrs. Cuthbert, the housekeeper, promptly chased her out of the room.

For a couple of days, Nanny ambled aimlessly around and then finally managed to get back outside, whereupon she made for the flowers again. This time Mr. Watts saw her first.

And so President Lincoln sat down to compose a letter to his wife. The first two sentences concerned family financial matters, and then the letter continued:

"I suppose you are glad to learn this. Tell dear Tad,

poor Nanny goat is lost, and Mrs. Cuthbert and I are in distress about it. The day you left, Nanny was found resting herself and chewing her cud on the middle of Tad's bed. But now she's gone! The gardener kept complaining that she destroyed the flowers, till it was concluded to bring her down to the White House. This was done and the second day she had disappeared, and has not been heard of since. This is the last we know of poor Nanny."

The departure of Nanny by no means brought an end to Tad Lincoln's string of pets. There was always Nanko. And Tad found other interests. He expressed a desire to raise pigeons; nobody objected to this except the White House caretakers. The birds multiplied rapidly and did the type of damage pigeons had long been noted for.

Then there was the matter of a turkey named Jack, which a family friend sent to the White House to serve as the First Family's 1863 Christmas dinner. Tad wasn't aware of the bird's ultimate fate—to him Jack was one more pet to have fun with. Tad and turkey became great pals, with Jack following the boy everywhere he went.

But shortly before Christmas, Tad found out the dinner menu and ran sobbing and wailing to his father. The President was in the midst of an important meeting, but he always had time for Tad. He listened to his son's tearful plea, then hastily wrote some words on a card. It was a reprieve for the turkey, who soon became a White House fixture.

The turkey came to the President's attention again later

under much more pleasant circumstances. During the 1864 election, soldiers stationed in Washington were permitted absentee votes at a special facility set up on the White House grounds. The President, Tad, and Noah Brooks, a noted newspaper reporter for the Sacramento *Daily Union* (later Lincoln's private secretary), were at the window peering through the rain at a line of soldiers waiting to cast their ballots. Suddenly Jack strutted in among them.

"Why is your turkey at the polls?" the President asked his son. "Does he vote?"

"No," replied Tad, flashing a bit of his father's famous wit, "he is not of age yet."

It was a story Mr. Lincoln repeated with a grin to many of his associates.

When President Lincoln was killed by an assassin's bullet, his body was brought back, along with that of his son Willy, to be laid at rest in his hometown, Springfield, Illinois.

The story of Lincoln and his son's pets would not be complete without a word about Fido, the dog who was left behind. Fido did not attend the funeral march, although Old Bob, the Lincoln family horse, did.

At the gathering in the Lincoln home that followed the ceremonies, Fido was permitted to move through the throng. Never did any dog receive more caresses than this ordinary dog whom the Lincolns so loved.

The yellow-brown mongrel lived on for one year after

Lincoln's burial. Then, when he was playing outside the Rolls' house, a drunk came staggering by. Always friendly, Fido leaped up on the man, no doubt trying to greet him. The drunk, frightened, drew a knife and stabbed the dog to death.

Fido—also assassinated—was buried in an unmarked grave in the back garden of Abraham Lincoln's home in Springfield, Illinois.

Chapter 6

A SCOTTY NAMED FALA

FOR many people, there are two symbols of those heroic years of World War II. One is a man wearing a shapeless fedora, its brim upturned, a cigarette holder stuck in his mouth at a jaunty angle. The other is a small black Scotty, his ears pointed skyward, a perpetually quizzical expression on his face.

President Franklin Roosevelt was really an expert on the subject of dogs. He seldom accepted a dog as a gift, preferring to select pets himself. He did receive numerous dogs as gifts, but kept comparatively few of them. The rest were either returned to the senders with thanks, or given away to friends. One of the first things President Roosevelt noticed during his initial tour of the White House grounds was the kennels. They were then located where the East Wing of the building is now, and he thought it a rather hot place for them. Probably it is not generally understood that temperatures around the White House can climb high, high, *high*. So the Roosevelt dogs were not kept in the kennels, but allowed to roam the grounds and the house itself, causing some anguish to the people who had to clean up after them.

When President Roosevelt's Administration began, his favorite dog was Major, a buff-and-black German shepherd, one of several police dogs he owned. That dog tried the President's patience from the moment he was let loose to run around the lawn. Major had one disconcerting trick he probably learned as part of his police dog training. He would walk up to a visitor, take the startled person's wrist firmly between his jaws and scrutinize his face carefully. Fully half a minute would elapse before he would finally release his hold and allow the visitor in. The so-called fake bite terrified many of the President's friends. Mr. Roosevelt didn't think it partcularly amusing, either.

There was nothing fake about the bite Major took out of Senator Hattie Caraway's leg. Nor was the dog pretending when his sharp teeth ripped the trousers of British Prime Minister Ramsay MacDonald when he came to Washington on a state visit. After a third person felt the sting of Major's teeth, the dog was kept chained to a doghouse.

Somehow, Major stayed in hot water throughout his brief White House residence. Once he came out of his own special nook under the spiral South Portico staircase, limping badly. Mrs. Roosevelt thought it was just a strain, and tried to nurse him herself. For more than a week, she hovered over the shepherd, changing the compress often.

When Major showed no signs of improvement, Dr. David E. Buckingham, the White House veterinary, was called in. Dr. Buckingham put the dog through a series of X-rays and found that he had a broken leg. How the leg was broken was a complete mystery. No sooner had Major recovered from that injury than he was back in the hospital again. This time the vet discovered a number of painful cysts growing on the dog's back. It was the type of ailment that would not ordinarily be suspected, except by a trained vet. An operation was performed, the cysts were removed, and Major spent some time recuperating in the private kennel of Dr. Buckingham.

At first, it was thought that Major's biting was the result of those cysts. After all, any animal might snarl and snap if it were in pain. But that did not prove to be the case at all. When he returned to the White House, apparently hale and hearty, Major resumed biting people as though he had never been away. This time he sank his teeth into a hand of a passing Washingtonian, who had put his hand through the fence to pat Major on the head.

That was it—the shepherd was banished.

Major was not the only Roosevelt dog who harassed humans. Another such was a Scotch terrier named Meggie, who was brought to the White House when she was eight years old. The Scotty was Mrs. Roosevelt's dog and for a time was peaceful enough. When taken for a walk, she would usually bark for one block's worth of exercise, then settle down and conduct herself with decorum. For some reason Meggie liked to sleep in fireplaces. Perhaps the feel and smell of ashes made her comfortable, but it certainly made her dirty, and Meggie loathed the baths that necessarily followed.

Meggie flashed her fangs just twice too often. She bit the well-known *New York Times* Washington reporter Bess Furnam on the nose and soon afterwards bit both Sistie and Buzzie Dall, the President's grandchildren. The dog was given to Dr. Buckingham, who reported that the change of scenery apparently settled her down, for she was no trouble to him.

Still another biter was Winks, a young Llewellyn setter presented as a puppy while the President was vacationing in Warm Springs, Georgia. Winks had the habit of biting anyone handy—guests, attachés, and others, although he never bit too hard and there was really no malice in the dog. He was simply a prankster. To him it evidently seemed like a funny thing to do. People usually forgave him, especially when they heard about the incident of the disappearing breakfasts. On this particular occasion, a breakfast had been prepared for the President's domestic staff. The food, consisting of bacon, eggs, and toast, was placed on the table so that the staff could serve themselves. The kitchen was unoccupied while the cook stepped out to summon everyone to breakfast. The door was left open, and Winks happened to be passing by. The heavy aroma of hot bacon and eggs was too much for him. Since there was nobody to stop him, the dog fell to with gusto, and in just ten minutes, every one of the nineteen plates had been licked clean.

When President Roosevelt was told what had happened, he roared with laughter. He commented, "The only reason the dog didn't wash it down with coffee was that it hadn't been poured yet."

In July, 1933, suddenly Winks was dead. It happened quickly, catching everyone by surprise. He had been romping merrily across the lawn in the company of Pal, a bulldog belonging to a Roosevelt aide. Perhaps it was the heat, or perhaps it was an accident. Witnesses said that Winks suddenly staggered, careened, and crashed headlong into the iron fence. The severe concussion killed him almost instantly. Winks was buried in Rosedale Dog Cemetery at Silver Springs, Maryland, not far from the grave of Manchu, the spaniel belonging to Alice Roosevelt Longworth. President Roosevelt was on a Pacific cruise when the accident took place. Mrs. Roosevelt was also away. Only Dr. Buckingham and Meggie, then ten years old, stood at the graveside when the pine box was lowered into the ground. Winks had died before he was a year old.

Pal, too, was affected by the heat. One humid day he suddenly ran amok on the South Lawn. Those who witnessed the scene thought at first glance that he might have suddenly gone mad, and Dr. Buckingham was hastily summoned. Pal meanwhile had leaped into a fountain pool. There was no water in it at the time, and he was lying motionless when the vet arrived. Pal was not mad, simply a victim of the heat. He eventually recovered.

The heat problem caused President Roosevelt to think twice before accepting another dog he took a fancy to. This was Tiny, a large, shaggy English sheepdog. The President thought that Tiny would be happy at Warm Springs, but later realized that it would be unwise to send such a heavy-coated dog to such a warm climate. Tiny was turned over to a close friend, Admiral Cary T. Grayson, who was later his doctor.

For the time, Winks was replaced by a lovable Great Dane puppy offered to the President by ten-year-old Jackie Greenway, son of Isabel Greenway, the new representative from Arizona. Jackie had already named the pup President. With so friendly and winning a gift-giver, and a dog so aptly named, Mr. Roosevelt could hardly refuse the gift.

All those dogs were newsworthy enough, and no doubt they gave President Roosevelt a great deal of pleasure. Their biting caused him concern, but having known dogs all his life, he knew that some dogs might nip a stray hand when provoked by strangers, or even by members of his own family. Life in the White House could hardly be called peaceful, what with people streaming in and out constantly, photographers popping flashbulbs, and the confusion of voices from every side.

It was not until the last year in President Roosevelt's second term that his most famous dog entered the White

House. In the spring of 1940, a cousin of the President, Margaret Daisy Suckley, received a black Scotty puppy from a friend, Augustus Kellogg, of Westport, Connecticut. Miss Suckley presented the dog to her distinguished relative. Born on April 7, 1940, the son of Peter and Wendy, the puppy had been named Big Boy. After one look at the puppy, the President changed its name to Fala. With typical Roosevelt humor, he said he was honoring on obscure Scottish ancestor known only as "Murray the Outlaw of Fala Hill."

With the exception of Warren Harding and Laddie Boy, no President and dog ever shared so deep and abiding a love. Only death could and did part them.

Fala made himself at home immediately. He usually slept on a Navy blanket in the President's bedroom. When he played outdoors, it was within sight of the Executive Office window, from which Mr. Roosevelt would watch his dog. During the cocktail hour, the President's favorite time of the day, he could heave a huge sigh and let the tension drop away for a few moments. Fala could be fed a few choice morsels, but only after he rolled over, sat up and begged, and performed one of half a dozen other tricks that delighted his master.

The two were all but inseparable. When the President took a drive in his car, Fala could be seen perched on the seat beside him. When the President went to his home in Hyde Park, New York, Fala went, too. If Mr. Roosevelt felt the need to go to Warm Springs, Georgia, to bathe and exercise his paralyzed legs in the soothing, sulphur-bearing water, he would take Fala. The Scotty proved to be something of a nuisance to the Secret Service men—not because of anything he did, but because his mere presence revealed that the President of the United States was in the neighborhood. They debated the advisability of asking the President to leave his dog at the White House, but decided against it, knowing full well the request would be turned down flat. Where the President went, the dog would go—it was as simple as that.

In little more than a year, Fala progressed from a national to an international symbol of United States dogdom. When a "war dog" drive for funds was begun, Fala became an Army Private by contributing one dollar. His picture with the Commander-in-Chief, Mr. Roosevelt, appeared everywhere. Countless other dog owners followed suit. In August, 1941, Fala's photograph appeared in almost every newspaper in the free world. Under a cloak of the tightest secrecy, the President had boarded the U.S.S. *Augusta*, which sailed into the North Atlantic. There the so-called Atlantic Charter was drawn up. Fala accompanied his master and had his picture taken as he lay at the feet of two of the world's most important men, President Franklin D. Roosevelt and Prime Minister Winston Churchill.

Fala was also unlike Franklin Roosevelt's previous dogs in that instead of being the biter, he was often the bitten. Fala received thousands of love letters, now in a section of the Roosevelt Library at Hyde Park. Scotty owners everywhere wanted pups who could claim Fala as their father.

The President thought it over and decided it might not be a bad idea for Fala to have offspring.

Once more Daisy Suckley entered the scene. She suggested that her one-and-a-half-year-old female Scotty Buttons and Fala be introduced on a summer visit to Hyde Park. So they were. However, this was not a match made in heaven, for no sooner did Fala tentatively approach his bride-to-be than she snarled, lashed out, and sank her teeth into the would-be groom. Fala beat a hasty retreat with as much dignity as he could muster under the circumstances, but it was evident that the courtship was over before it had begun.

One newspaper reported that he had been hospitalized. This was not the end of it. Some time later a local veterinary in Fishkill, New York, in a news conference at his animal hospital announced that Fala and Buttons had been brought together in a remote-control mating by means of the test-tube method. He was happy to report that two Scotty pups had been born and that they had been named Meggy and Peggy.

Years later, after President Roosevelt had died, Fala was even more severely mauled by Blaze, Elliott Roosevelt's gigantic mastiff. Blaze was the same dog that had become notorious during World War II when a homeward-bound G.I. was "bumped" from a plane so that Blaze could be taken aboard instead.

The mastiff's attack on the Scotty was unprovoked. Fala had been ambling amiably across the Hyde Park lawn when Blaze suddenly and savagely tore into the smaller dog, inflicting such deep wounds that many stitches were required. Because the onslaught had been so unexpected and so vicious, it was feared that rabies might be the cause of Blaze's attack, so the mastiff was destroyed. A post-mortem revealed that Blaze did not have the disease. When Mrs. Roosevelt was questioned about the incident, she was annoyed and bluntly told reporters that this was a private family matter.

There is no record of Fala's having bitten anyone. He did like to nip at a small doll that squeaked when he clenched it between his teeth, but that was as far as he went.

As the years passed, Fala continued to be a political asset as well as a Presidential companion. On one occasion, Mr. Roosevelt sailed to Hawaii for an important conference. Because of wartime quarantine restrictions, Fala was not permitted to go ashore, and although it would have been simple to make an exception in his case, the President refused to ask special privileges for his dog. Fala was left aboard ship. The crew took a liking to the Scotty and they fed him gladly—overfed him, in fact. Once, one crew member cut off a lock of Fala's hair as a keepsake, and soon other sailors began snipping away, thinking the dog still had plenty of hair left. In practically no time Fala had a sizable bald spot. When the President returned to the ship and saw what had happened, he lost no time expressing his displeasure over the liberties taken with his dog. Newspapers in the United States gave the story quite of bit of space. Fala wasn't hurt, and the hair grew back rapidly.

The most celebrated political incident ever to involve a Presidential pet took place during the 1944 campaign. Once again Fala accompanied Mr. Roosevelt on a sea voyage. (The Scotty was certainly the all-time undisputed champion traveler in the history of White House pets.) Some political enemy circulated the story that on the return voyage, Fala was inadvertently left behind, and that the President had sent a destroyer to fetch the dog back. According to the rumor, the act of forgetfulness on the part of the President cost the taxpayers approximately fifteen thousand dollars. Now, no partisan politician would allow such a golden opportunity to slip through his fingers, and some Republican officials pounced on the story. The high-tax, spendthrift President had done it again, they shouted! Once more he had victimized the American people!

Unfortunately for the Republicans, Mr. Roosevelt was a past master at turning a seeming liability into a decided advantage. In one of his famous Fireside Chats, addressing the nation by radio, he denied the story and proceeded to point out why this attack on his dog was unwarranted.

With wonderful Roosevelt sarcasm, he said, "These Republican leaders have not been content with attacks on me, or my wife, or on my sons. No, not content with that, they now include my little dog, Fala.

"Well, of course, I don't resent attacks, and my family doesn't resent attacks, but Fala *does* resent them.

"You know, Fala is Scotch, and being a Scotty, as soon as he learned that the Republican fiction writers in Congress and out had concocted a story that I left him behind on the Aleutian Islands and sent a destroyer back to find him—at a cost to the taxpayers of two or three, or eight or twenty, thousand dollars—his Scotch soul was furious. He has not been the same dog since.

"I am accustomed to hearing malicious falsehoods about myself—such as that old, worm-eaten chestnut that I have represented myself as indispensable. But I think I have a right to resent, to object to libelous statements about my dog."

And then—with bewildering swiftness—Fala's beloved friend was gone. On that day in April, 1945, Fala was sitting quietly watching his master having his portrait painted in Warm Springs when his master slumped over the papers he was signing. The President was carried into his bedroom by Arthur Prettyman, his valet. The dog watched with uncomprehending eyes as secretaries, aides, and doctors scurried in an out. A hush descended over the cottage.

Suddenly Fala knew. He leaped up, shaking violently, then went crashing through a screen door, barking loudly and frantically. As fast as his scrubby legs could take him, he raced up a nearby hill, where for a long time he stood vigil, refusing to return when called.

Fala returned to Washington with the body of his master, but now he was subdued, with a resigned composure that spoke volumes. Just before the funeral, newsmen later reported, a steady howl could be heard, but it came from a retriever belonging to one of the late President's grandsons. It howled mournfully outside the East Room, where President Roosevelt's body lay in state.

Inside, the mourners stood quietly in the heat, and I remember the heavy scent of the banks of flowers as we listened to Bishop Dun. I don't remember hearing the dog howling.

In an outpouring of emotion, people everywhere extended their love for the President to his dog. Fala continued to receive numerous gifts, letters, and invitations—many of them addressed simply to "Fala, Hyde Park, New York."

Mrs. Roosevelt and Fala spent a good deal of time together, taking long walks in the woods overlooking the Hudson River or sitting quietly while she wrote or visited with a few friends. Between them was a mutual respect, but as the President's widow often said, "Fala was always my husband's dog. He merely accepted me."

Eleanor Roosevelt, too, took the dog on frequent trips. Once a hotel in Maine refused to accept Fala as a guest because of a strict no-dogs-allowed rule. Mrs. Roosevelt had not known about the rule. Instead, she went to a tourist cabin that permitted dogs to sleep in a guestroom. As she reported in her famous syndicated column, "My Day," she did not blame the desk clerk for barring Fala. "The clerk was quite right to stick to the rule," she said, "and I have no complaint."

Fala died in April, 1952. It was a mercy death. The twelve-year-old Scotty had been in failing health for some time and at the end had become too feeble to eat. There was nothing else that could have been done for him. He had outlived his master by seven years. Fala lies buried in the Hyde Park rose garden, and he is resting as usual in his place near his master.

Chapter 7

ANDREW JACKSON'S THOROUGHBREDS

As a rule, when generals became Presidents, they had rewarded their faithful old battle chargers with an easy life in some grassy pasture. George Washington "pensioned off" his Nelson and Blueskin. Generals Taylor and Grant petted and pampered their military mounts as long as the animals lived.

Andrew Jackson's wartime mounts that had carried him through the battles of the War of 1812 were long gone when he took office in 1829. Those horses, though he was fond of them, were never his true favorites. He appreciated their sturdy constitutions and courage and the way they stood firm under the barrage of cannon and rifle fire. However, another type of horse was his real enthusiasm.

Old Hickory was "an improver of the breed," a student of past performance charts, a follower of the Sport of

Kings. He was a devoted fan of racing. So, when Andrew Jackson became President, he had three racing fillies in his stables, Emily, Lady Nashville, and Bolivia. They weren't just for show, either. These horses were entered in many a competition, though never under Andrew Jackson's name or colors. The owner of record was his son-in-law, Andrew Donelson. This was done in order to quiet the possible criticism that it was not proper for a President of the United States to keep race horses.

Mr. Jackson had been an admirer of pure-bred horseflesh for many years before he became President. As a youth he saw his first racing meet, and his interest in a good thoroughbred never wavered. He had come to Tennessee from the Carolinas with two blooded horses and had begun to race them almost immediately. Whether as the owner of an entry or as a mere spectator, Andrew Jackson could be seen at all the important meets, casting his experienced eye on the fillies and young geldings. He read many books on all aspects of horses as well as watching them in action. One of his biographers said of him, "He knew all about the noble animal, from pedigree to pathology." Jackson could, when necessary, perform some of the veterinary's duties.

In 1804, after resigning as judge on the Tennessee Superior Court, Jackson decided to go into the business of breeding thoroughbreds at "The Hermitage," his Tennessee plantation. To sire his colts, he wanted the best racehorse that money could buy, and that meant Truxton, a magnificent stallion owned by Major John Verrell, a noted sportsman of the day. To scout his proposed purchase, General Jackson attended a match race between Truxton and Greyhound, an outstanding racehorse belonging to Mr. Lazarus Colton. Greyhound won, but the general could see that Truxton wasn't handled properly and was not in the peak of condition for that race.

He arranged for a return match between Truxton and Greyhound to be held at Hartsville, Tennessee. The purse: five thousand dollars. It was a tremendous occasion in local turf history. People flocked to the track from all parts of the county to witness the race. According to Mr. Douglas Anderson, who recorded the details in his *Making the American Thoroughbred,* excitement was at fever pitch. He said, "No contest on the soil of Tennessee has ever been so exciting or caused so much betting, considering the means of the people, as this race. Hundreds of horses and numerous 640-acre tracts of land were staked on the results. The old pioneers bet on Greyhound with the utmost confidence."

Andrew Jackson staked his wagers on Truxton. He knew in his heart that he was the better horse, and he was right. Truxton beat Greyhound. General Jackson took home his share of the winnings—a part of the purse, and also as a result of an unusual personal bet, about fifteen hundred dollars worth of wearing apparel. Several of Mr. Jackson's friends, realizing the general knew how to pick the winner, wagered the same way and went home with a great deal of money and deeds to land. General Jackson bought Truxton and put him out to stud at the Hermitage.

The Turf Register cites an article written by Jackson for *The American Farmer,* in which he stated:

"Truxton is a beautiful bay, full of bone and muscle; was got by the imported Old Diomed and came out of the thoroughbred mare, Nancy Coleman. His performances on the turf have surpassed those of any horse of his age that has ever been run in any western county; and indeed, it might be said with confidence that he is equal if not superior to Mrs. Ball's Florizel who now stands unrivaled in Virginia as a race horse. Truxton, by sportsmen and judges, is admitted to be amongst the best distance horses they ever ran or ever had to train. His speed is certainly known to all those who have run against him."

Truxton's value to the general was considerable. He won a number of high stake races. Records indicate that he was never beaten in a two-mile race during his prime, and he was also the sire of some four hundred colts, some of whom won many races.

It was said that Jackson had only to look his champion squarely in the eye and tell him "Win!" and the race was as good as over. Jackson made many influential friends as he became known throughout the area as a breeder of champion horses. Wealthy sportsmen came to "The Hermitage" to purchase breeding stock and later some of these men became important political allies.

General Jackson and Truxton formed a kind of man-and-horse mutual admiration society. Every evening the General would visit his stable; horse and owner would enjoy this short visit. As the stallion grew old, he grew unruly and crochety, even as people do. The stable boys were sometimes unable to cope with him, but a nuzzle, a caress, a whisper from his master, and calm would prevail.

Indirectly, Truxton was the cause of one of the duels fought by Jackson. The incident began when a race was scheduled between the great two-miler and another notable thoroughbred named Ploughboy, owned by Captain Joseph Erwin. The stakes were two thousand dollars, with an eight hundred dollar forfeit if either horse failed to compete. Perhaps Captain Erwin realized that his Ploughboy was no match for Truxton, or there may have been other reasons for withdrawing his horse. At any rate, Captain Erwin paid the forfeit money, and the race was canceled.

Mr. Charles Dickinson, Captain Erwin's son-in-law, was also a horse breeder. The story goes that he was jealous of Jackson and angry that the race was not run. In his opinion Ploughboy was unbeatable. That night after the race was called off Mr. Dickinson was in a local tavern where he repeated some unfortunate remarks about Mrs. Jackson's not having been divorced when she married Jackson. The general was completely devoted to his wife and would fly into a terrible rage when he thought someone had slandered her.

Because Jackson was a friend of Captain Erwin, the

general asked him to silence his son-in-law. There was no reason to slander an honorable woman. Mr. Dickinson apologized but the incident must have burned within him, for he repeated his remarks on another occasion.

Now the general was in no mood for forgiveness. The two men fought a duel in which Jackson was wounded and Dickinson killed.

Rachel Jackson died shortly before the first Inauguration of her husband. Soon there was a different Rachel Jackson in the White House, the daughter of his adopted son Andrew, Jr., the "Beloved little namesake of my wife."

Rachel and Andrew Jackson had adopted Andrew, Jr., one of twin sons born to her brother's wife, when he was a baby. He grew up as their own son. All told, the Jacksons raised eleven children of relatives and old friends at "The Hermitage," and six of them lived in the White House during Andrew Jackson's tenure of office. Andrew Jackson took greater care of the children than most real grandfathers would do. He would walk them when they had the colic, would stay up with them when they were nervous or worried. He adored children and always wanted a lot of them around him.

Despite all of his affairs of state, Jackson never forgot his affairs at "The Hermitage." One of his concerns was the welfare of Poor Poll, Rachel's pet parrot. William Donelson was the custodian of the parrot, and after one of the President's departures from "The Hermitage," he wrote to him, "Poor Poll is doing well. She is as fat and saucy as ever. From her continued good health, I think she will live to be an old bird. Elizabeth [William's daughter] desired to be remembered affectionately to you and says that she will insure Polly's health until your return."

Jackson wasn't entirely satisfied with William's assurances about Poor Poll. Soon after returning to the White House for his second term, he wrote Billie Donelson:

"My dear Sir:

Write me on receipt of this and let me know how your dear little Elizabeth is and whether Poor Poll, favorite bird of my dear wife is still living."

It is recorded that when Jackson died at "The Hermitage," Poor Poll distinguished herself by introducing an element of the grotesque into the solemnity of the funeral services. She suddenly startled the assembled mourners by bursting into a loud torrent of profanity that made it necessary to suspend proceedings until her perch could be removed from the upper front portico to a more remote point.

Thomas Hart Benton tells of his visit to Jackson's home in the book *Thirty Years' View*:

"I arrived at his house one wet chilly evening in February and came upon him in twilight [this was long before he was in the White House] sitting alone before the fire, a lamb and a child between his knees. He started a little, called a servant to remove the two to another room, and explained to me how it was the child had cried because the lamb was out in the cold and begged him to bring it in which he done to please the child, his adopted son, then not two years old."

Old Hickory was an old sentimentalist where children were concerned.

Chapter 8

THE CALVIN COOLIDGE
COLLECTION

IN a sense, with the passing of President Warren Harding, two celebrities were lost to the nation. Not only did the American people suffer the loss of a handsome and likable President, but also, with the departure of Laddie Boy, a newsworthy national pet was gone from the Washington scene. The Airedale had been a marvelous subject for the capital's correspondents. When events of the day were comparatively dull, he was always good for filler copy, or even a short feature article. Some of the reporters wondered what kind of replacement, if any, the new President would bring to the Executive Mansion.

On the front page of *The New York Times*, Saturday, August 18, 1923, the headline said, "Mrs. Harding Quietly Leaves White House. Laddie Boy Greets Coolidge Warmly."

The New York Times reported, "President Coolidge is

not inclined to be superstitious, but something occurred last night when he and Mrs. Coolidge went to the White House to call on Mrs. Harding that he regarded as a good omen.

"When the Presidential automobile drew up under the porte-cochère before the north door, Laddie Boy bounded out and down the steps in greeting so cordial and affectionate that both Mr. and Mrs. Coolidge took special notice of it. Mr. Coolidge, relating the incident to callers today, said that he hoped it might be regarded as an omen of the spirit in which he might be received by all those associated with the late President." *

A few days later in *The New York Times,* another front-page story described how the Coolidges moved into the White House on Tuesday, August 21, and went on to say:

"Laddie Boy continues to romp around the White House although it is said there is a rivalry among some friends of the late President to become his owner. The former red bow in his collar has been replaced with a black one. He has not yet worn the silver collar made for him by admirers in Alaska." †

To a great extent Calvin Coolidge was unknown. In 1923, long before the "in-depth" interviews by radio and television correspondents, few people knew much about his personality. Mr. Coolidge was so extremely economical

---

* *The New York Times,* August 18, 1923. © 1923 by The New York Times Company. Reprinted by permission.

† *The New York Times,* August 22, 1923. © 1923 by The New York Times Company. Reprinted by permission.

with words that he was soon dubbed "Silent Cal." When he had nothing to say, he said nothing. When there was no news to report, he reported none. In that respect he was a very untypical Chief Executive.

When we lived in the White House, we heard from the household staff more stories about Calvin Coolidge than about any other President. One very amusing story concerns his efforts to get away from the Secret Service when he wanted to take a walk. He went out a different door every morning. They finally had to station a man at every door in the Mansion, and believe me, there are quite a few doors in that house. But he never got away from them.

Within a very few months, it was evident that Mr. Coolidge, his charming wife, and his two sons, John and Calvin, Jr., were second to no previous First Family in their love for animals. Probably Theodore Roosevelt was the only President to accumulate around him as wide a variety. The years of the Coolidge Presidency were one long procession of pets; some stayed at the White House only briefly; others remained for quite some time, and got their pictures in the newspapers.

During this pet parade, the nation learned that Mrs. Coolidge had a delightfully whimsical way of her own when it came to selecting animal names. Furthermore, when occasion demanded, she was not above changing a name already bestowed on an animal.

A short time after the Coolidges moved into the White House, they were given two warbling Harz Mountain canaries, which Mrs. Coolidge named Nip and Tuck. Soon several additional birds were added: Snowflake, a chirping white canary from California; a thrush named Old Bill; Goldy, a yellow bird of indeterminate origin; a tropical bird whose previous owner had trained it to swoop down suddenly on some unsuspecting person's shoulder and nip his ear.

Mrs. Coolidge also had a mockingbird like some earlier First Ladies, but she released it when she learned that a Washington, D.C., law made it illegal for anyone to keep mockingbirds in cages—the penalty, a five-dollar fine or a month in jail. The birds were pleasant but they created no more than a passing level of interest.

The tempo began to pick up when cats arrived. The first was a foundling, a gray-striped alley cat who wandered into the White House grounds through the iron fence and decided to stay for a while. Tiger, as the President called him, was a hostile creature who just didn't like people, especially photographers who were continually poking cameras in front of his whiskers.

Tiger tolerated the President, and Mr. Coolidge took a liking to the cat, probably because he recognized an independent spirit when he saw one. Visitors would often come upon the President sitting on the porch with Tiger on his lap.

This cat was a wanderer at heart, and one day he just walked away as suddenly as he had arrived. The President was quite upset. He poked around the grounds, demanding of the guards, "Have you seen my cat?"

Tiger's disappearance was so disconcerting that Mr. Coolidge asked the local radio station to broadcast a description of Tiger, with an appeal that the finder return him to the White House. Tiger was picked up later at the Navy building. However, Tiger got out again, and this time he stayed lost.

The second cat was Blacky, who had belonged to a nurse in Waverly, Massachusetts. When she had no room for him, she shipped Blacky to the President. It may sound strange to ship an unwanted pet to the President of the United States, but it seemed that anyone who had an animal he wanted to get rid of sent it to 1600 Pennsylvania Avenue. Some came express collect, others prepaid, and a few were delivered personally. With good humor the Coolidges accepted them all. Many of the ordinary animals were given to friends. All the more exotic ones were sent to the zoo. Mr. and Mrs. Coolidge kept a few. Blacky was one they retained for a while.

Just as Tiger had been a wanderer, Blacky was a hunter. No sooner had he made himself at home in the White House than he began a reign of terror throughout the grounds. He went after squirrels, rabbits, and birds, doing so much damage that he was banished to the guardhouse by the front gate.

Blacky stayed there until the nesting and mating season was over, then was let out. As if highly miffed over such treatment, he ran away. Unlike Tiger, he came back of his own accord; evidently he knew a good thing when he had one. The President was not particularly pleased about Blacky's return. He had been fond of Tiger, but he never did care for Blacky.

The era of the Coolidge pets went into high gear when the dogs began to arrive. The first to reach the White House was Peter Pan, a wire-haired terrier. He was a gift of Dr. Alonzo G. Howard of Boston, Massachusetts. In an accompanying letter, Dr. Howard expressed the wish that the dog's education would be completed by Mr. Coolidge.

Peter Pan did not last very long. He was not the friendliest of dogs. He snapped at people and in general showed a surly disposition. He did exhibit a marked preference for Edward T. Clark, one of the President's secretaries, and Mr. Clark eventually became the dog's master. Moral: If you're a Presidential secretary, "Don't let the dog get fond of you or you may wind up with the dog."

Then into the White House came Laddie Buck, half-brother to President Harding's beloved Laddie Boy. After a few days of keen observation, Mrs. Coolidge changed his name to Paul Pry, because this was one of the oddest dogs ever to sniff around a White House corridor. When asked a specific reason for the change of name, Mrs. Coolidge replied that he seemed to have his nose in everybody's business. Paul Pry just seemed to fit perfectly.

The dog became devoted to his mistress, sleeping in her room, and nobody, but nobody, could venture through the door while Paul Pry was on guard. Once Mrs. Coolidge was about to take a short trip when she discovered that she had forgotten an article in her room. She sent her maid to fetch it. When the luckless girl crossed the threshold, Paul Pry leaped across the floor and bit her.

Mrs. Coolidge doted on Paul Pry, probably for the same reason some women take a liking to a bad boy. She would take the "dear rascal" shopping, first muzzling him and attaching a strong leash to his collar. Store owners were very glad to see the First Lady, but were a good deal less enchanted by a visit from her dog.

When his manners and disposition continued to deteriorate, Paul Pry was sent to a Marine Corps detachment, for it was thought that by becoming a "devil dog" he might learn some discipline. He stayed only briefly as the Marines weren't crazy about him, either. The dog was then given to Captain Andrews, skipper of the Presidential yacht, the *Mayflower*. The captain took him home, but that didn't work out, either. Andrews said he had to lock him up every time he spanked his children—otherwise he'd lose an arm. Finally Paul Pry was returned to the Marines. The President declared that they were the only people as tough as that erratic dog.

A few months after Mr. Coolidge assumed the office of President, a pet arrived destined to replace Laddie Boy in the hearts of the American people. A beautiful white collie was presented to the President. It was true love at first sight. His name was Oshkosh, and he was born at the Island White Kennels in Oshkosh, Wisconsin.

His first masters were a farm family, and Oshkosh was a trained sheep-and-cattle herder. Even-tempered and dependable, the collie was the kind of working dog his ancestors had been—marvelous with other animals, he was especially adept at driving cattle to and from the pastures. In dry weather when pastures were shortened, the time for the cattle's homecoming was moved up to mid-afternoon. In only three days, Oshkosh had somehow memorized the new timetable. On one occasion, the cows came home without the dog and it was thought he had failed to perform his duty. But in a little while he showed up with the maverick in tow. Oshkosh had barked and pushed and prodded the calf till it got the idea and headed toward home.

The collie had a typical dog's reaction to water. Back on the farm he used to jump on the running board of the family truck and go with the boys to an old swimming hole, where he enjoyed a good splash. But when he came to the White House, Oshkosh shied away from taking a bath. Of course, once he was bathed and dried and combed to a silky softness, the collie strutted as though he were the most beautiful creature on earth. And there was no question that he was indeed a magnificent specimen.

Mrs. Coolidge, too, appreciated the dog's appearance. She decided that Oshkosh was no name for a dog of that quality. She rechristened him Rob Roy, after a highland outlaw in a novel by Sir Walter Scott. Like Laddie Boy, Rob Roy was permitted to attend important meetings, as well as to join interviews by foreign and domestic correspondents. Usually the collie was placid enough. He would bark inquisitively at a caller he didn't know but then become quiet the instant the President spoke to him. When satisfied that the person was harmless, he would lie down at a safe distance, following the flow of conversation by turning his head in the direction of each speaker.

Only once did he break up a meeting temporarily. During a crowded news conference, Rob Roy began to whine incessantly in a high plaintive tone. Mr. Coolidge soon saw what was happening and spoke sharply, "Will you newspapermen kindly keep your big feet off my dog's toes?" When he was no longer stepped on, Rob Roy fell silent again.

Rob Roy had one trick that would delight the President, and he also had one bad habit that caused great concern. The trick: Mr. Coolidge would place a piece of cake on the mantelpiece so that its edge just protruded over the ledge. Rob Roy would rise up on his hind legs and nudge the cake gracefully until it started to fall. He would then lunge and catch the cake in midair.

The bad habit was chasing cars. The President was afraid that someday his collie would get too close to an automobile's wheels. Vice President Charles G. Dawes offered one solution: tie Rob Roy to a stake at the end of a 30-foot rope. The dog would race after a car and would then be brought up sharply when he reached the end of the rope. With two or three stiff neck jerks he would get the message and surely the bad habit would be cured. The President vetoed that idea for it might break his neck at the same time.

A story I remember being told by my father is of Senator Morris Sheppard of Texas. Senator Sheppard was invited to breakfast at the White House one morning. He noted the beautiful collie wandering around in the dining room. The collie was very well-behaved and would come and sit down and look at him, as though he were trying to tell him something. Finally President Coolidge said to Senator Sheppard, "He wants your bacon." So Senator Sheppard gave the collie his bacon. He got no more bacon —the Senator, I mean, not the dog.

For a time, Rob Roy ruled the roost as the number one dog at the White House. Then came another beautiful white collie, a fitting companion in every way. Prudence Prim, as Mrs. Coolidge named the female collie, was truly a heart-stealer. Although she was a large dog, Prudy never did enjoy robust health, and so was not too playful. She was rather the affectionate type with great soulful eyes and a lovely face, gentle of disposition and soft of voice.

Just as Rob Roy was the President's dog, Prudence Prim belonged to Mrs. Coolidge, and the four of them could often be seen together taking a stroll around the grounds. The First Lady lavished a great deal of time and affection on Prudy. She even designed and made a large floppy straw hat trimmed with lots of ribbons that the collie wore to a garden party. Dog and hat were a triumph of fashion, and this was repeated on several other occasions. No doubt Rob Roy sensed that Prudence Prim was in delicate health, and he seemed solicitous of his playmate. They made a handsome couple and were constantly surrounded by photographers. They appeared in newspapers and magazines hundreds of times.

Neither collie was destined to gladden the Coolidge's White House base for very long. In the summer of 1926, while accompanying her mistress on vacation to the Black Hills, Prudy fell ill and died. After Prudy's death, the joy of living seemed to leave Rob Roy. He became fretful and mournful, and lost his appetite. On September 23, 1928, two years after Prudy, Rob Roy also died, a victim of ulcers.

The President was disconsolate. Mrs. Coolidge also felt the loss keenly. Even though Prudence Prim had been her dog, she had her portrait painted with Rob Roy alongside her.

To ease the pain of the collies' passing, two children in Orion, Michigan, sent a replacement. An airplane delivered a Shetland sheepdog named Diana of Wildwood. But airplane travel in the mid-1920s was not the clean, fast means of transportation it is today. Poor Diana arrived covered with grease from tail to muzzle, so much so that the first newspaper account described her as a black-and-white spotted dog. When she was bathed and the grease was scrubbed off, it was found that Diana was almost entirely white with just a few stray brown spots.

After that ordeal Mrs. Coolidge decided that Diana was hardly a suitable name and a new one was given—Calamity Jane. Playful, good-natured, and so happy that her name was almost changed to Jolly Jane, Calamity enlivened the severe White House with her clowning. This included quick nips at the heels of Tiny Tim. Tiny Tim was a really good-sized reddish-brown chow. He came as a puppy, but in two months he turned out to be not so tiny. In almost all respects he was the opposite of Calamity Jane. The sheepdog was a yipping friendly animal, while Tim was aloof, enigmatic, and—it had to be faced— a grouch. For a time, Mrs. Coolidge debated about changing his name to Terrible Tim.

Dogs came into the White House in endless procession. There was Blackberry, a chow who liked to howl. He would bay mournfully at the moon, at the ceiling, at trees —anything. The office of President of the United States is difficult enough without having to hear the constant howling of a dog with a single-track mind. Blackberry got on Mr. Coolidge's Republican nerves and was finally given to the daughter of the Governor of Connecticut. He must have been a Democrat.

Ruby Rough was an affectionate brown collie. Some White House aides took to calling her "Foxy" or "Mule Ears," but never within Mrs. Coolidge's hearing. Boston Beans was a small bulldog and he remained at the White

House for a very short time. This was the one dog with whom Prudence Prim would frolic, but then the games she played were somewhat on the cruel side. Beans tried to join the romping of the other dogs, chasing after them on his stubby legs, trailing his leash behind. Prudy let the small bulldog work up a full head of steam, and then grabbed the leash in her mouth, causing poor Beans to take a spill and roll across the lawn.

Other dogs included King Kole, a black Belgian police dog; Bessie, a yellow collie; and Palo Alto, who had been trained as a bird dog before being given to the President.

One of the President's most interesting pets was a furry raccoon sent by some constituents in the state of Mississippi. The raccoon was intended for Mr. Coolidge's Thanksgiving dinner, but Mr. Coolidge never entertained any such culinary ideas, and the raccoon was in no danger of being eaten. In a very short time, the raccoon had acquired a name, Rebecca, plus a large pen built near the President's office.

Rebecca and the President hit it off immediately. They would take long evening walks together, with the raccoon waddling along at the end of a leash. It got so that the President never let a day go by without a brief visit with Rebecca. He would stop at her pen and watch as she played happily in some water, swishing around a bar of soap, creating a layer of dirty suds.

When the Coolidges moved temporarily into quarters in Dupont Circle, while the White House was being repaired, Rebecca had to be left behind, since there was no room for the raccoon. Unable to look in on his pet, the President began to fret. He worried about her well-being. Was she being well fed? Did she have enough soap to play with? One afternoon, a limousine drove into the grounds, moved through the workmen, and stopped at Rebecca's pen. The President got out, led Rebecca into the car, and drove back to Dupont Circle, where he spent a brief hour playing with the raccoon. After that Rebecca was boarded out at the zoo until repairs at the White House were completed and the First Family and the raccoon were returned to a normal routine.

Ever a practical soul, the President reasoned that a female raccoon needed a male raccoon, and so Horace, a wild denizen of the woods, was brought to keep Rebecca company. It soon became evident that the two animals had better be kept apart, at least at the beginning. Horace was a sulky loner who despised captivity. He was as mean as Rebecca was gentle. No amount of pampering or cajoling would change him.

Mr. Coolidge ordered a new pen built, complete with a log house, where Horace could pout in comfort. A great Norwegian spruce tree stood in the middle of the cage, transplanted there especially for the raccoon's climbing practice. That tree proved to be Horace's way out. The wild animal found that by swinging out at the end of one particular branch, he could drop clear of the cage. The first time he tried it, a White House policeman saw him and recaptured him. The limb was trimmed by several feet, but that made no difference; Horace managed to escape again—not once, but twice. The last time, he disappeared for good.

Rebecca, too, left hearth and home for one night. Nobody knows why she suddenly decided to go, how she left, or what she did. She was finally located at the State War and Navy Building. For a time, Rebecca was in disgrace, but eventually the President forgave her.

The canaries, the cats, the dogs, and even the raccoon were all placed in the capable hands of Willie Jackson, who had taken care of President Harding's Laddie Boy, and he seemed to have a way with animals. Mr. Coolidge had the greatest respect for Mr. Jackson's talents, but was not above teasing him on occasion.

The President was soon to receive a pair of lion cubs, a gift of the mayor of Johannesburg, South Africa, so he asked Willie whether he knew how to care for lions and he hinted that he wanted them chained. Of course, the pet overseer was understandably nervous about such an assignment, and his associates, thinking to pacify him, suggested that the President was only joking. Willie knew better, insisting, "if he was fooling, he sure can look serious and honest."

Willie vowed to do the best he could, providing the lions were still young and not too ornery. He then asked the President if he thought the lions would fight. With a perfectly straight face, Mr. Coolidge said that they were quite playful and that one of them had bitten off a man's foot. "However," he added, "that wouldn't have happened if the man had been smart enough to keep his foot on the ground."

"Oh, it was off the ground," sighed Willie. "Then, that man must have been doing some running."

The lions arrived, and fortunately for Mr. Jackson, they were dispatched to the Washington Zoo.

The cubs were among the hundreds of other pets Mr. Coolidge shipped to the zoo. Among them were a wallaby, a small hippopotamus, a vicious bobcat, and a cinnamon bear. The pigmy hippo had been captured on the rubber plantation of the President's friend Harvey Firestone, in Liberia. It was one of only three such hippos in the United States when shipped into the country. About the size of a large dog, it was extraordinarily frisky and became quite a favorite at the zoo, where it lived well into the 1960s.

The bear, which was fond of marshmallows, was presented to Mr. Coolidge in 1923. It was captured in Oklahoma by Colonel B. R. Rearson, who placed it in a large van and drove it to Washington, accompanied by the Oklahoma City Brass Band. Mr. Coolidge walked out onto the lawn to receive the gift, listened patiently to the speeches and the music, thanked the Colonel, and when they were out of of sight, turned the beast over to the zoo.

The President was mystified when told of the impending arrival of a wallaby. He had no idea what a wallaby was and called the zoo's curator, who told him it was a kind of a kangaroo. The wallaby, a gift from an American living in Tasmania, carried its young in a pouch, fought with its tail, and jumped in order to run. The President pondered the difficulties of keeping such a creature on the grounds, and finally gave up the idea when someone pointed out that the marsupial might leap over the fence, get into the street, tie up traffic and who knows what else.

Smoky, the bobcat, was the largest of its type ever captured in its home county in Tennessee and was sent by the Great Smoky Mountains Association. The President wanted no part of that snarling, spitting bundle of dynamite, but he had to take it, for a very good reason. The county in which the dear little fellow had been captured was the tightest Republican stronghold in the entire United States of America. Exactly four hundred fifty-two votes had been cast there during the Presidential election, and Mr. Coolidge had received four hundred forty-two of them.

Calvin Coolidge and his wife managed to endure all these gifts with good grace. They thanked those who presented Ebenezer the donkey, and the antelope, and they never batted an eye at a flock of chickens that ended up staying in the President's bathtub because there wasn't anywhere else to put them. Nor did they grow flustered when actress Marie Dressler sent them a big white goose while they were vacationing at Swampscott. They knew it was an obvious publicity stunt. Miss Dressler was then appearing in a Broadway play titled *The Goose Woman,* and the show's press agent swore that this goose was worth a hundred thousand dollars. If it was, then a lot of money was wasted when someone left the door open and Enoch—that was what Mrs. Coolidge named it—was out and flying high over the Atlantic Ocean, disappearing fast.

The two Coolidge boys, being in school, were not often at the White House. Calvin, Jr., was there during the summer of 1924, and then one of the great White House tragedies occurred. During a tennis match, the sixteen year old wore a blister on his foot. Blood poisoning set in. The distressed President, knowing how much the boy loved animals, caught a rabbit on the White House grounds and took it to his son to distract him while he was confined in bed. The boy, too ill, soon died. It was the first death of a child in a First Family since that of Willy Lincoln, almost sixty years before.

Chapter 9

A GOAT, A COW,
AND WILLIAM HENRY HARRISON

THE first Benjamin Harrison served as a member of the
Virginia legislature before, during, and after the Revolution. He was a member of the Continental Congress
and one of the signers of the Declaration of Independence.

His son, William Henry Harrison, soldiered with dis-
tinction in the Shawnee uprising at Tippecanoe and in the
War of 1812. He became the ninth President of the
United States. The slogan of his election year of 1840 was
a famous one in history, "Tippecanoe and Tyler, too."

President Harrison's grandson, the second Benjamin
Harrison, commanded a Union Army brigade that saw action at Kenesaw Mountain, Peach Tree Creek, and Nashville. He became our twenty-third President in 1889, between the two administrations of Grover Cleveland.

President Benjamin Harrison was the man who is re-
sponsible for all the confusion about how many Presidents

there have been and which number each President has. Everybody tries to count Cleveland twice, as the twenty-second *and* the twenty-fourth President, which my father thinks is nonsense, and I agree. There are just so many bodies, and you ought to count only them.

Both Benjamin Harrisons were serious, politically intense men, but not so William Henry. Genial and friendly, the middle Harrison was an unassuming man—the type who enjoyed doing his own marketing. He was always ready to trade banter with a stranger about politics, the price of corn, or the weather. He was also a doting, devoted grandparent during his brief stay in the White House. (He died after only one month in office.) When he became President, William Henry Harrison's children were grown and married, but there were grandchildren—the future president Ben, his younger sister Mary, and another granddaughter, Marcina.

President Harrison's grandchildren were eager White House visitors and, whenever possible, enjoyed playing games on the spacious lawn. Like any grandfather, the President was always trying to find new and amusing gifts for the youngsters. One day the children ran out to begin their usual activities, only to find a billy goat hitched to a new red wagon, awaiting their pleasure. Naturally, they were delighted. Ben took over the driver's seat, and the two girls took turns standing behind him as he drove the wagon for hours, each trip around the grounds being more enjoyable than the previous one.

The new arrival was looked upon with great prejudice by the Harrisons' coachman, Willis. He took one look at the goat and decided he didn't like him. The goat didn't like him, either. The first day's meeting produced almost immediate fireworks. The goat was quartered in the stable. Willis entered. The goat saw his enemy, lowered his head, and charged. Willis took out as fast as he could, with the billy goat in hot pursuit. The coachman vaulted over the cart, reached a fence near the carriage entrance, and climbed up to straddle it. When Willis attempted to climb down the other side, the goat, showing surprising presence of mind, ran through the gate and stood there with horns lowered at the ready, waiting for his adversary to get within butting range. The commotion drew several of the White House staff to the scene. Two gardeners sneaked up close, collared the goat, and led him away.

Freed of his tormentor, Willis sought an audience with the President and issued an ultimatum: either "His Whiskers," as Willis called the goat, left the premises without further delay, or he'd quit!

The President didn't want to take away his grandchildren's new pet, but at the same time he considered the services of Willis to be quite valuable. Finally a compromise was reached. As long as Willis and the goat kept out of each other's way, future clashes could be avoided. The goat was removed from the stables and provided with quarters of its own under the rear portico.

Normally, the goat was quite placid with the children,

but something bothered him one day and "His Whiskers" decided to seek the great wide world outside. It wouldn't have been so bad, except that young Ben was in the cart at the time. The President was on the porch, waiting for his carriage, when the goat dashed by with the cart and Ben.

"Stop!" cried President Harrison. When the goat paid no heed, the President gave chase. Boy, cart, and goat sped out onto Pennsylvania Avenue with the Chief Executive of the land, wearing a high silk hat, frock coat, and waving his cane, running along behind them. At last the goat slowed sufficiently for the President to catch up. With a gasp of relief, he snatched his grandson from the cart, hugging him fiercely. "Are you hurt, Ben?"

"Why, no, Grandpa," replied the puzzled child. "That was a fine ride. I liked it."

The story of President Harrison and the cow was published in 1926 in a book titled *Twenty-five Years of White House Gossip* by Edna M. Coleman. Variations of the story were known for many years, but Miss Coleman said she discovered it in a newspaper clipping that was pasted in an old scrapbook she came across in a second-hand bookstore. The name of the newspaper is not given and Miss Coleman candidly admitted that she had no idea whether or not the article was published before that. In any event, I think it is an amusing story.

A native and old resident of Washington tells the following anecdote that was current and credited in Washington during the brief administration of President Harrison, who was called "the Cincinnatus of the West" by the Whigs and "Granny Harrison" by the Democrats.

When he came to Washington to be inaugurated, no one was surprised by the plain looks and the simple manners of the old hero, because the pictures of the log cabin in which he had lived were common during the campaign as illustrating his simple habits. No, nor were they incredulous at the story they soon heard of him.

It seems that there was no cow—or no satisfactory cow— at the White House, so the old ex-farmer made inquiries and learned that Saturday was the day that the drovers came in from the country to the Marsh Market to sell their cattle. Consequently, early one Saturday morning, President Harrison, instead of sending a servant, arose and walked down to the market. There he found cows "galore"! He soon made a trade with a burly Montgomery County drover by which he became the possessor of a fine Durham [Suki by name].

"Where shall I drive it, sir?" inquired the drover, who did not recognize the President.

"To the White House. I will show you the way," replied the President.

"Why you don't mean to say, friend, that you've bought this yere beast for old Granny Harrison?" demanded the drover with wide eyes.

"Yes," replied the old hero, without showing the resentment that a smaller man might have felt necessary.

The drover left his cattle in the care of his son and turned the Durham out on the avenue. He and the President walked side by side behind the cow, guiding her way. The President on the inside raised his stick gently when Suki made an effort to promenade the sidewalk and the drover flourished his whip when she threatened to break into the middle of the street.

"I'm a Democrat, myself," the drover volunteered to his companion, "and voted for old Van"—Van Buren, of course—"but the other day, at the 'nauguration—ha, ha, ha—I'll be doggoned if I didn't fling my hat and hurrah for Granny Harrison with the best of 'em! Couldn't help it somehow."

"Thank you," said the President.

"Oh, you're a Whig! But I might a-known that by your having a siteration at the White House, as I s'pose you have, h'ain't you?"

"Yes," said the President.

"What be you there now? Gardener?"

"No."

"Coachman then, or bodyservant?"

"Neither. I suppose I may call myself a general servant."

"Oh yes! Run errands, wait on the table, answer the door-knocker and the like o' that?" remarked the drover, who had no idea what the domestic establishment of the President of the United States was like.

"Something not very unlike that," said the President with a tolerant smile.

"Do you see much of Granny Harrison now?" inquired the man as he neared the White House grounds.

"Considerable," replied the President.

"How do you like the old fellow?"

"That's hard to tell. Too well, most likely," thoughtfully replied the old hero.

"I'll go bail you do!"

"Well, here we are," said the President, opening a gate that led to the stables. Several menservants came forward, touching their hats.

"Take charge of this cow and attend to her," ordered the President. Then turning to the drover he said, "Come, friend, come to the house and have some breakfast."

"Thank ye, I don't care if I do. Say, could you get me a sight of old Granny Harrison?"

"Didn't you see him at the inauguration?"

"Lor', yes, but not nigh enough to know what he looked like! I'd like to get a squint at him, anyways!"

"Come in, friend," said the old soldier, leading the way up the steps and through the south door into the mansion.

The drover turned around and looked out upon the extensive grounds, and then remarked, "A better place than that ar log cabin out in Ohio."

"I don't know about that," replied the old soldier, leading the way along the hall. Here they were met by a servant dressed like a clergyman who bowed and opened a door to the left. The President ushered his guest into the family breakfast room, where breakfast was standing ready.

"Lor'-a-mighty what a sight of silver and chiny!" exclaimed the drover, gazing on the glittering service.

Here were more servants, who, with deep bows, placed more chairs at the table.

"Sit down, friend," said the illustrious host, politely indicating a chair.

"Looka here! I say now! Ain't you taking on a great liberty? Granny Harrison wouldn't like this here now, would he?" inquired the drover, puzzled and hesitating.

"I think he would, very much. Pray sit down."

"And just look here, now! Ain't you too fresh?" inquired the drover with his hands on the back of the chair, which for some reason or other he did not take. "Who be you anyhow, as to make so bold and take such liberties in the President's house? You ain't told me your name, nor likewise your siteration here as gives you so much freedom."

"The people call me William Henry Harrison, and have made me President of the United States," quietly replied the ex-farmer.

"Lord almighty!" cried the drover, and he bolted from the house and never stopped running till he was off the grounds when he sat down on the curbstone and "cussed himself gray" as his wife said.

It is unfortunate that William Henry Harrison's term was so short—the shortest, in fact of any Chief Executive, lasting only thirty-one days. He was struck down by pneumonia and became the first President of the United States to die in office. Almost fifty years later, grandson Ben took up the burdens of the Presidency, and it is more than likely that on several occasions he stood looking across the green lawns toward the gate through which he had ridden in a cart drawn by a runaway goat a few jumps ahead of his grandfather who loved him so dearly.

Chapter 10

HERBERT HOOVER'S WATCHDOG

Protecting the life of the President of the United States and his family is a full-time job. Whenever the President, his wife, son, or daughter takes a trip or is at home at the White House, Secret Service agents can be seen hovering discreetly in the background. Also, depending on the occasion, local uniformed policemen or detectives are assigned to guard the First Family. Security is very tight, with the White House police on the outside and the Secret Service on the ground floor and the main floor inside the White House.

Evidently President Herbert Hoover's police dog, King Tut, did not trust so important a responsibility to Secret Service agents or policemen, although he was never really trained as an attack dog. He imposed this sentinel's duty on himself because of his incredible devotion to the President. Whatever the reason, King Tut took his watchdog assignment seriously—so much so that it eventually cost him his life.

President Hoover's dog became known around the White House as "the dog that worried himself to death!"

Mr. Hoover had acquired King Tut some years before he became President, while on a trip to Belgium as a war relief organizer in 1917. The dog seemed to be happy enough before his master assumed the post of Chief Executive, and gave no inkling of the ferocious devotion he was to exhibit later. Nor was Tut the only pet the Hoovers kept in those pre-Presidential days. Mr. Hoover served as Secretary of Commerce in the early '20s and lived at 2300 S Street in Washington, D.C. Mr. Hoover's son, Allan, was extremely fond of animals and usually had an interesting collection of pets in and around the house. He attracted birds into the yard by placing food and water in the trees and by hanging gourds on branches to serve as living quarters. To Allan, two cats and two dogs were the irreducible minimum of household pets, although the number seldom went that low. For a while he kept two ducks, which waddled across the yard and sat on the porch. Someone gave the boy two alligators, which he added to his collection of land turtles. Mr. Hoover and his son had a hassle or two about the alligators as he tried to convince the boy they belonged in the bathtub at night and should not be left wandering around loose.

Although Mr. Hoover was quite satisfied to see his son become deeply involved in nature study, he himself was first and foremost a dog fancier. He raised no objections to other dogs being kept in the house, or later on White

House grounds, as long as it was understood by everybody that King Tut was strictly his dog.

In the eyes of some animal lovers, Mr. Hoover got off on the wrong foot almost from the start. Shortly after his inauguration in March of 1929, he ordered the closing of the official White House stables. It was a puzzling move to many Washington observers. The President did not dislike horses—he could ride well—but he pointed out that horses had seldom been used except for riding since the time of Theodore Roosevelt.

President Taft had done some riding on doctor's orders as a weight-reducing measure, but not very much. President Wilson was very rarely seen in the saddle. President Harding was on record as having ridden exactly twice— once in Washington and again while visiting the mountains near Hagerstown, Maryland. President Coolidge, although quite familiar with horses, having raised them on a farm, was not much of a horseman, and rarely climbed aboard one of the available mounts. There were seven horses "going to waste," and four men employed to take care of them. Since neither he, nor any other member of the First Family, had any intention of riding, what was the use in keeping them? So the horses were returned to the Quartermaster stables for redistribution, and the four men were no longer needed.

Actually, President Hoover closed the stables solely as an economy measure. In another money-saving direc-

20. Fala sat in front of FDR, beside Churchill, on the U.S.S. *Augusta* when the Atlantic Pact was written in mid-ocean.

21. Fala, the most famous of White House pets, fathered these two pups after their mother bit him. He himself was always gentle.

22. Meggie and Major, Mrs. Roosevelt's dogs. Both made headlines by biting prominent people. Newspaper woman Bess Furman was a victim.

23. FDR's dog Winks stole 18 breakfasts in the White House staff dining room. Here he shows how he did it, for the newsmen.

24. Hoover was known as a "cold" politician—this picture with his dog, King Tut, was distributed before election to show his humanity.

25. Coolidge dogs often made the news, as their wild animals did. Headline: "What Is to Become of White House Pets when Coolidges Leave?"

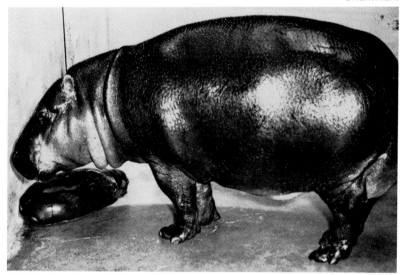

26. A gift to the Coolidges, this pigmy hippo, with its tiny baby, became the most popular animal in the Washington Zoo.

French Collection, Library of Congress

27. When the Coolidges received these two South African lion cubs, the President somberly asked his White House gardener to train them.

28. A raccoon was sent for the White House Christmas dinner, but Mrs. Coolidge adopted it instead and the President cared for it.

29. When we moved to the White House, this portrait of Grace Coolidge and Rob Roy was my favorite. Painted by Howard Chandler Christy.

30. Laddie Boy, Harding's Airedale, became the most powerful dog in national affairs. He sat in a chair at Cabinet meetings.

"I HOPE SECRETARY DAVIS WILL GRANT ALL THE WATCHDOGS AN EIGHT-HOUR DAY."

31. In this famous newspaper "interview," Laddie Boy gave his opinions on the entire Cabinet, Alaskan mail dogs, and such.

32. In support of the war effort, Woodrow Wilson saved expenses by keeping sheep to cut the lawn.

33. Each day, rain or shine, Theodore Roosevelt went riding on Bleistein—Here they go down Penna. Ave.

34. Kermit with his terrier Jack. The dog was always bedevilled by the cat Tom Quartz, who chased him everywhere he fled.

35. Algonquin, Archie Roosevelt's Icelandic pony, was the most photographed family pet. Here they appeared on the White House driveway.

36. Taft's White House cow, Pauline, grazing on the South Lawn, with the stately State Department building in the background.

37. President Benjamin Harrison kept a goat for his grandchildren. His grandfather, President William Henry Harrison, kept a goat for him.

38. Tad and Willy Lincoln had ponies, but after Willy died, Tad was a lonely little boy, and seldom went riding.

tive, Mr. Hoover decommissioned the Presidential yacht, *Mayflower.*

Those and several other acts helped project an image of Herbert Hoover that was not the real Herbert Hoover. The President was really a warm, compassionate human being, but few bothered to find out the true nature of the man. In the eyes of many of his constituents and even a number of officials in the Republican Party, he seemed to be a machine, obsessed with cold logic, interested only in fact-finding, statistics and reports, surveys and figures. This was the argument presented by some against his nomination for the Presidency. In a way, it was King Tut who helped Mr. Hoover win the nomination of his party.

One day a Hoover supporter came across a photograph of the man and his dog. It was an informal pose, taken at his residence on S Street, showing Mr. Hoover smiling as he held his pet up by the forepaws. In a frenzy of inspiration, the party official had thousands of those pictures printed. That snapshot became valuable campaign material in a drive to humanize Herbert Hoover. It was placed in newspapers and magazines and enlarged into life-size posters. Autographed copies of the photo were sent to thousands of admirers.

That picture alone did not really make a President, but there's no denying that it helped a great deal.

During King Tut's residency there were several other dogs on the White House grounds—some with enviable pedigrees and long records of prizes won at dog shows:

Patrick, one of a pair of large, majestic wolfhounds, was so huge that people peering in through the gate mistakenly thought that they were ponies. Big Ben and Sonny were friendly, white-haired fox terriers. Glen was a handsome Scotch collie. For a time the Hoovers owned an Eskimo dog named Yukon, but he became so lonesome for the north country that the President had to send him back.

The canine group also included a truly beautiful setter named Eaglehurst Gilette. Mrs. Hoover's particular favorites were Pat, a police dog, and Weejie, a frolicsome little elkhound from the famous Hemson Kennels at Ski, Norway. Mrs. Hoover simply doted on these dogs. A photograph of Mrs. Hoover and her favorites appeared on her 1932 Christmas card with the handwritten greeting, "From Lou Henry Hoover, Weejie and Pat."

There were other White House pets during Herbert Hoover's Administration, but only one other caused a stir, and then only for a few days. It seemed that one spring day a possum strayed on the grounds and was found by the President. Such arrivals are always good for a paragraph or two in the newspapers and the possum's arrival was duly noted along with a picture of the animal. Mr. Hoover grew rather fond of the creature. Meanwhile, the possum mascot of a school baseball team in nearby Hyattsville, Maryland, had suddenly vanished. As the distraught boys went hunting for their living symbol of good luck, they noticed the picture of the President's possum. Some-how it looked suspiciously like their own wandering Billy, and possibly it was—who knows? Of course, only young boys and other similar experts might be able to tell one possum from another. In order to make sure, a delegation of several of the school's athletic leaders came to the White House to identify the possum.

However, the animal flatly refused to be identified and no amount of coaxing could get him to leave the kennels.

No doubt, one has to be a member of a successful base-ball team to realize the true worth of a good luck mascot. The situation presented a stickly problem of protocol. The boys couldn't very well come out and say,

"Hey, Mr. President, did you swipe our mascot?"

First of all, Mr. Hoover hadn't swiped the possum—it had wandered in of its own accord, and since the possum stayed put in its hideout, they couldn't identify it posi-tively. Soon it was all smoothed out to everyone's satis-faction. The boys left a note with one of the President's secretaries, saying that they would like to have the Presi-dent's possum to counteract any bad luck in the event their own possum was found by their opponents. That was very diplomatic.

Mr. Hoover responded by presenting the animal to the boys from Hyattsville, and it is a matter of record that the Hyattsville baseball team reached the state championship series.

With so many dogs to play with, and no rival in sight, King Tut's life should have been one continuous romp. But things didn't work out that way, and the misfortune was all his own doing. King Tut paid no attention to the other White House dogs. From the beginning, he took it upon himself to maintain a constant vigil, lest some nameless person were to sneak in and do harm to his master or mistress. No other living being, human or canine, could protect hearth and home to his satisfaction. This was a job he had to do himself.

Every night, in good weather or bad, White House guards would come upon King Tut patrolling the fences. The dog would stop at each gate and checkpoint. If it was time for the guard to change, he would look around anxiously, waiting for the relief guard. King Tut usually knew the special police and guards by sight or sniff. No one could fool him. If a new man showed up, the dog made it his business to get acquainted so that he would know him the next time they met.

Many of the White House aides thought it amusing that King Tut should assume such a heavy responsibility, but the dog was in deadly earnest, and there was no humor in him as he wandered from post to post checking up on the personnel. In that respect, King Tut himself never had a fixed post. He was considered by Richard Jarvis, chief of the White House Secret Service, to be a sergeant, rather than just another sentry.

King Tut never slept, or so it seemed. During the day

he would take short naps, but these were restless and fitful and his constant nighttime patrol duty left him no real sleep.

Concerned about his faithful pet, the President tried to stop him from going out so that he could rest, but Tut would have none of that. He would bark and yelp till he was let out. Once through the door, he would resume his self-appointed rounds.

King Tut was unlike most of the other dogs who lived in the Executive Mansion in that he could never adjust to the normal routine of White House life. Yet, there were chores other than guard duty that he performed for his master during the day. He would trot up the steps with the newspaper clamped in his teeth. When the President chose to read the paper out of doors, it was King Tut's job to sit on those sections the President had finished reading, to keep them from blowing away.

As the weeks and months passed, the rigorous day and night life began to tell on aging Tut. He became morose, he sulked, lost both appetite and weight. Actually he became something of a hypochrondriac, whining and whimpering for no apparent reason. Towards the end of his canine dictatorship over the White House grounds, it was painfully evident that he had fallen into bad habits. He became distrustful of the guards. It was not safe for workmen to show themselves in the rear grounds.

At last it came out that he couldn't stand the sight of anyone near the White House except the President and

Mrs. Hoover. Now the canine watchman had to be watched, lest he attack innocent people. The now thin, ill-tempered dog could have done real damage to human flesh. At first he was muzzled, but that only seemed to aggravate the situation. Finally, as there was no longer any way to control the dog, he was sent back to the S Street residence. There was no master, no mistress to protect here. Puzzled, King Tut pined away and soon was dead.

President Hoover did not release the news of Tut's removal back to S Street and his death until some months had passed. He knew that gift dogs might be sent to the White House, and he was in no mood for that. No other dog could have taken King Tut's place. The stock market had crashed, the country was sinking into a depression, and those matters were uppermost in his mind, not a new pet.

Chapter 11

BUTCHER BOY AND THE GENERAL

PRESIDENT Grant's kindest critics called him a naïve Chief Executive, and probably he was. Some friends he appointed became involved in political scandals. But the great general showed in his character those qualities he most admired: loyalty to friends, even when ill-used by them, courage, and discipline.

Mr. Grant's deep-rooted respect for living creatures—predators as well as domesticated animals—was undoubtedly the result of his early years on a farm. Many of his biographers cite the boy's God-given gift for silent communication with all the animals in the barnyard, though he had almost no pets as a child.

On a visit to Mexico, he felt a distress and concern that one might not expect in a fighter used to the pain of war. He recorded the scene in his autobiography:

"Every Sunday there was a bull fight for the amusement of those who would pay their fifty cents. I attended one of them—just one—not wishing to leave the country without having witnessed the national sport. The sight to me was sickening. I could not see how human beings could enjoy the sufferings of beasts, and often of men, as they seemed to do on these occasions. . . . I confess that I felt sorry to see the cruelty to the bull and the horse. I did not stay for the conclusion of the performance."

The same sympathy was extended to the wildest, most savage creatures. On his round-the-world tour, Mr. Grant stayed for a while at the dazzling palace of the Maharajah of Jaipur and received an invitation from his host to accompany him on a tiger hunt. As diplomatically as possible, Mr. Grant begged off. In his book, *Men and Memories,* John Russel Young wrote of this incident. Not even the Maharajah of Jaipur, with his many elephants and multitude of hunters, could persuade Grant to chase and kill the tigers.

Grant's abiding passion was always horses. He told one amusing anecdote about himself as a child that reveals his early sensitivity, and also his horsemanship, which many historians believe was his means as a youth of combatting his shyness. In this episode, his father allowed him to go buy a colt he very much wanted.

"I at once mounted a horse and went for the colt. When I got to Mr. Ralston's house, I said to him: 'Papa says I may offer you twenty dollars for the colt, but if you won't take that, I am to offer twenty-two and a half, and if you won't take that, to give you twenty-five.' It would not require a Connecticut man to guess the price finally

agreed upon. This story is nearly true. I certainly showed
very plainly that I had come for the colt and meant to
have him. I could not have been over eight years old at
the time. This transaction caused me great heart-burning.
The story got out among the boys of the village, and it
was a long time before I heard the last of it. Boys enjoy
the misery of their companions, at least village boys in
that day did, and in later life I have found that all adults
are not free from the peculiarity."

At West Point, he was easily the best rider in his class,
and his outstanding feats of horsemanship were also much
in evidence during the Mexican campaign and later in
the Civil War.

He knew the value of horses, as was evidenced at Ap-
pomattox, when he permitted the defeated Southern soldiers to keep their mounts for their transportation home
and for farm work.

Mr. Grant was not content merely to be in the saddle.
He admired and enjoyed all sorts of horseraces—either as
spectator or participant. He always had an ambition to own
a trotter—a desire he expressed on any number of occasions. Often he tried his hand at driving the well-known
trotters and pacers owned by notables of his acquaintance.
Once, Mr. Vanderbilt loaned Grant his famous Maud S.
which Mr. Grant later described as "the finest mare I ever
drove."

During the Civil War, General Grant had ridden a
smallish but spirited black horse, whimsically named Jeff

Davis, after the Confederate President. He also owned another, perhaps more dependable, saddle-horse named Cincinnatus, presented to him by the people of Cincinnati during the early years of the war.

When he became President, Mr. Grant took both horses to the White House, but he probably favored Cincinnatus, for he chose that horse as a model for an equestrian statue in front of the Capitol Building.

As President, Mr. Grant never owned birds, but there's one story about a large number of canaries that describes the campaign era of that time. It was planned that following Grant's Inauguration a large gala ball would be held in a building hastily erected for that purpose on Judiciary Square. It was truly an enormous, if jerry-built edifice, with the main ballroom reportedly measuring 300 feet long by 150 feet wide. There was no such structure around in my day. As a symbol of the nation, a large wooden American eagle was hung from the ceiling, with streamers attached to it, stretching to all corners of the room. An arrangement of gaslights was designed to resemble a sunrise. The highlight of the Inaugural was to be the canaries, hundreds of them being suspended in cages from the ceiling. It was planned to have the Marine band play "Hail to the Chief" as President Grant entered the ballroom. At a signal, the band would cease playing. It was assumed that the canaries, primed by the music, would sing to gladden the heart of the new Chief Executive. Unfortunately, the weather that night, in early March 1869, was less than cooperative. A sudden freeze enveloped Washington, much like the blizzard that hit the Inauguration of John F. Kennedy. The chilled canaries were far more interested in finding warmth than in singing. Not a peep was heard from any of them.

Three birds did reside at the White House during the Grant Administration. Señor Romero, the Mexican minister, presented son Jesse with a parrot, and as he related in his book, *In the Days of My Father*, "this parrot had no speech and was less noted for his beauty that for the violence of his temper. One might have imagined him nurtured on chili peppers. I kept him for years and then he was passed on through a succession of owners. Although I lost track of him long since, I should be surprised to hear that he is not still living." *

Jesse also owned magnificently colored gamecocks, and his description of them is very amusing: "Confined in adjoining yards, they fought continuously between the pickets. There was no chicken wire in those days. Then, when separated widely, each spent most of the daylight hours crowing challenge and defiance at the other." †

Jesse had a completely normal, small boy's desire to own one of everything in the line of pets, but since limits had to be imposed, he settled for dogs mostly. He did receive a number of dogs as gifts, but they seemed to die

* Jesse Grant, *In the Days of My Father* (New York: Harpers, 1925). Reprinted by permission of Harper & Row.
† *Ibid.*

quite mysteriously. This happened to several in rapid succession. Jesse remarked that, in his first days in the White House, his only sorrows were the deaths of these pets.

Then someone gave him a Newfoundland that won his heart. It was a fine specimen, playful and frisky, and Jesse voiced his fears to his father that perhaps this one was fated to go the way of the others.

"When this dog came," Jesse wrote, "Father called the White House steward. He asked no questions, made no accusations.

" 'Jesse has a new dog,' he said simply. 'You may have noticed that his former pets have been peculiarly unfortunate. When this dog dies, every employee in the White House will be at once discharged.'" [*] Faithful, as Jesse named the Newfoundland, enjoyed superb health throughout President Grant's tenure in the White House. So did the other dogs Jesse subsequently acquired.

For a while, Jesse wanted to raise pigeons, and he was disappointed that he was not allowed to. He discovered that Tad Lincoln had had the same ambition, and that the caretakers of public buildings in Washington were still trying to exterminate thousands of descendants of Tad's flock. No wonder pigeons were taboo to young Jesse!

The President seemed interested only in horses. During the first months he was in office, there were seven horses in the White House stables, and two Shetland ponies belonging to his sons, Buck (Ulysses, Jr.) and Jesse. The

[*] *Ibid.*

ponies, Reb and Billy Button, each pulled a little wagon with one small boy inside all through the streets of Washington. Nellie, the boys' older sister, owned two mares, named Jennie and Mary. A team of matched bays, named Egypt and St. Louis, were used on important occasions. Julia, a quick-spirited racer, was President Grant's favorite for a time, and of course Cincinnatus and Jeff Davis were given comfortable quarters after devoted service during wartime. Other horses were added later.

Several of President Grant's detractors complained that the seven large horses, not counting the ponies, were worth seven thousand dollars, which was a lot to spend for horses in those days. Of course, they were not worth that much, and Grant was heard to sigh and say he wished they were. Of them all, only Julia had any real value as a racer and she was by no means exceptional. Nor were any of the President's later trotters and racers.

If there was one thing the President dearly loved, it was a race. He delighted in driving around the racing track or speedway. In those post-Civil War days, the amateur sportsmen and horse fanciers in Washington enjoyed weekly events at a track, which was located in or near the neighborhood of what is now 22nd and H Street, N.W. Driving meets were a regular Sunday afternoon event, both winter and summer. In warm weather, the sulkies and racing carts congregated at the track in a festive, picniclike atmosphere. During the winter, the races were held even when snow and ice covered the track. Light sleighs replaced the usual racing rigs and the horses were rough-shod.

On this track, the President often tested Julia and some of his other horses. It took an important matter of state to keep him away. One evening, he was late leaving the White House, and cracked the whip to get to the track before everyone went home. Evidently there were speed laws in those days too, for a mounted policeman saw the horse and buggy moving rapidly along the boulevard and took out after it. The officer was new on the beat and did not recognize the President, and in the rugged manner of traffic policemen, he gave Mr. Grant quite a dressing down. Mr. Grant submitted meekly and later, when talking to an aide, insisted the officer be commended for doing his duty. He had been arrested for speeding but the charge was not pressed. Unless the President submits voluntarily, he cannot be arrested. I wonder if that's still true.

During the week, when the track was quiet, Mr. Grant would sally forth in his buggy, looking for someone else to challenge. He was usually given the right of way as he approached, and this was really the last thing he wanted. His horses were fast steppers, but sometimes the President managed to draw other wayfarers into racing against him. Twice he met rather ignominious defeats by delivery horses.

The first incident, reported by Grant's friend and personal physician, Dr. George F. Shrady, in his book, *Grant's Last Days,* involved a typical farm errand wagon. A farmer and his wife were returning from market. The President tried to overtake and pass the wagon, but every time he got close enough, the farmer would let out a shrill whistle and his horse would cut loose in a ground-eating elongated trot. The farmer stayed out in front for more than a mile, keeping well ahead of the President. Finally, he eased up to allow Mr. Grant to come within hearing distance.

"Did he know it was you, General?" the Doctor asked.

"Oh, yes," Mr. Grant admitted ruefully, "he knew. He said to me, 'General, you've got a good one there.' Then he moved on."

The second time the President ate dust, a butcher's delivery wagon did it. The wagon had stopped to make a delivery, and Julia passed it by. Soon the wagon passed the President again, stopped once more to make a delivery, and was at the curb while Mr. Grant cantered by. The procedure was repeated, and the President, sensing a race, happily put Julia into a gallop. Julia gave it a valiant try, but was unable to overtake the horse, until it stopped for good in front of the butcher shop. The President read the name on the wagon, returned later, bought the horse, and gave it a new name—Butcher Boy. He paid two hundred eighty dollars for the animal. Jesse Grant told an amusing story about the horse in his book: "A few days after acquiring Butcher Boy, Father was showing his new purchase to Roscoe Conkling. Conkling looked the horse over without a sign of approval.

" 'Do you know, General,' he said at last, 'I think I would rather have the two hundred and eighty dollars than the horse.'

" 'That's what the butcher thought,' said Father." *

Butcher Boy became the number one racer in the White House stable. It is said that the President looked hopefully for the farmer, hoping to meet him for another run down the avenue, but there is no record of such a return match taking place.

Chief groom of the stable was a happy-go-lucky man named Albert. Perhaps only he loved horses as deeply as the President. Quick-witted and extremely talkative, Albert would hold a running conversation with the animals. Sitting in on the seminar was Albert's dog—a black-and-tan mongrel named Rosie. Albert would take his dinner tray up to the stables and seat himself and have a cheerful chat with the horses, they nibbling hay while Albert relished his own food. To him, they were the world's finest table companions, probably because they never answered back.

Albert's proudest moments were those when he was driving the President in the large, heavy family carriage. For those occasions, the horses were curried and combed within an inch of their lives, the harnesses kept soft and

* *Ibid.*

supple, the metal gleaming, the carriage spotless. He maintained marvelous control over the horses. Albert allowed them to stamp and pull while waiting. No sooner did the President and Mrs. Grant put in an appearance than the prancing and fretting stopped. As Jesse described it: "The horses stood like statues."

Chapter 12

OLD IKE AND THE PATRIOTIC SHEEP

PRESIDENT Woodrow Wilson could hardly be considered the hearty, outdoor type. Studious and intellectual, the former president of Princeton University was more interested in a good book than in a good hunting trip. He did appreciate animals though, and had several dogs. His wife kept a canary or two but these ordinary pets seldom furnished unusual newspaper copy.

Mr. Wilson's main contribution to the world of White House pets was a flock of sheep and a tobacco-chewing ram named Old Ike. World War I was in progress. President Wilson wanted to stress the idea that citizens were expected to put patriotism before petty selfish motives. They were urged to pitch in by buying Liberty Bonds and conserving essential materials. And with manpower in short supply, what better way to keep the lawn trimmed, and thus do without extra gardeners, than by keeping a flock of woolly grass-eaters?

Dr. Cary T. Grayson, the President's personal physician, managed to round up a small herd of sheep. The entire flock of thirteen ewes led by the ram named Ike were brought to the enclosure on the South Lawn of the White House. To a certain extent, the sheep could be considered pets—the President did amble outside to inspect them from time to time, and he probably petted them as often as anyone else did. The sheep in turn were friendly enough, but if Mr. Wilson thought they would help the gardening situation he was totally, but totally, in error. They ate the grass all right, but also a great deal of expensive shrubbery and entire beds of exquisite perennials. How the White House gardener must have loved them!

However, the sheep were by no means a complete failure. Far from it; the flock was sheared periodically, the wool auctioned off, and the money donated to the Red Cross. It is reported that the shearings sold for ten dollars per pound and higher. One source credits the sheep with helping to raise one hundred thousand dollars for that worthy cause. The loss of a garden could be considered the President's own sacrifice in the name of the war effort, and he made many others.

In 1920, with the conflict fading from memory, the sheep were no longer useful. Not wishing to be bothered with another public or private auction, the President just gave them away. Mr. L. C. Probert, who was then superintendent of the Washington Bureau of the Associated Press, was the lucky recipient. Mr. Probert shipped them to his country place, which was called Homeland Farms located near Olney, Maryland.

Old Ike had been the subject of much attention during his stay at the White House. After all, a tobacco-chewing animal was something of a novelty. Yet he was not a one-of-a-kind freak. The field hands down South often fed rams and other animals a chew of tobacco for no particular reason other than that it amused them.

Ike was slow to pick up the habit, but once the nicotine took hold, he was hooked, just like any human cigarette smoker. When Old Ike wrapped his teeth around a wad of the weed, he would chomp away contentedly, with the tobacco flowing freely down the sides of his mouth, staining his lips and jowls an amber brown color. He might have been a human chewer except that people got rid of the wad when they were through with it. Ike swallowed his plug after it had been chewed to a mush. Ugh!

When he didn't have his tobacco ration, Ike would be a mighty unhappy ram. He was constantly begging for a bit of tobacco, any kind of tobacco from anyone who came near him. Mr. Probert was a cigar smoker, and that was just fine because Ike could sometimes pick up the stub when Mr. Probert was finished smoking it. The trouble was that Mr. Probert had his mind on other things, and feeding a hunk of tobacco to the Presidential ram was not always his first thought of the day.

One day as he was busy repairing a fence, Mr. Probert felt Ike nudging at his heels. He tried shooing the ram

136

away, but Ike wasn't about to be put off. Mr. Probert didn't realize that there was an unlighted cigar stuck in his mouth and Ike wanted a piece of it. Finally exasperated by the continual nudging, Mr. Probert delivered a stinging slap across Ike's nose and that, he thought, was the end of that. Moments later, as he was leaning over to drive a staple into the fence, Mr. Probert received a mighty blow from behind that knocked him head over heels over the fence. A lesson was thus learned by both parties. Probert didn't slap; Ike didn't butt.

The "Wilson flock" expanded rapidly. Ike was a father many times over, and the fourteen grew into a fairly good-sized herd of seventy. Mr. Probert didn't import any additional sheep. All were descendants of the few he started with. In 1926, Mr. Probert conceived the idea of having the wool made into blankets for several of his friends and former associates of President Wilson. It would be a lasting and practical memento of the wartime President.

Mr. Probert tried to find a manufacturer who would weave blankets of the wool. It had to be that wool and no other. The first few he approached would not honor the bargain. They would gladly make the blankets but not necessarily out of the wool clipping Mr. Probert sent. Finally one of the oldest blanket manufacturers and mill owners in the country agreed to do the job. Mr. Probert gave the blankets away in pairs. One set went to Dr. Grayson who had rounded up the sheep in the first place. Bernard Baruch got another set, and a pair of the blankets was presented to President Coolidge, then in office. There were plenty left, and Mr. Probert stored them away at his country house, keeping a few for himself and more handy in case they were needed for other friends. Unfortunately several months later, his home burned to the ground with the resulting loss of all the blankets.

President Coolidge, in a typical gesture, offered to loan Mr. Probert his pair, but only on a temporary basis. Mr. Coolidge liked those coverings very well indeed. They were just right for nights in the Adirondacks or the hills of Vermont. As a gesture he was even willing to forego their use in the Black Hills, where he prepared to go on a short vacation. But the President asked that the blankets be returned as soon as the next shearing could be woven.

As for Old Ike, he lived until August 1927, when, old and feeble, he was almost unable to rise from the ground. It was a mercy killing. But the thought of simply saying goodbye was a little too much for Mr. Probert. He wanted to give Old Ike one more treat before he passed on to his just rewards. So in those final hours, Mr. Probert offered Ike one last chew of strong tobacco, "eatin' tobaccy" as it was called. Ike took it eagerly. It was still in his mouth when he died.

Chapter 13

YUKI, BLANCO, AND THE BEAGLES

Any pain inflicted on a dog, deliberately or unintentionally, finds a horde of defenders ready to descend wrathfully on the perpetrator. President Lyndon B. Johnson learned this abruptly and to his dismay when he playfully pulled the ears of his daughter Luci's beagles while the press was present.

Certainly President Johnson had always been as knowledgeable about dogs as the average dog owner, and probably knew more about hounds than most.

Like everybody in the dusty hill country of Texas, he had his share of dogs, owning his first one, Rover by name, when he was three or four years old. He was a beagle admirer long before that breed became a fad.

Luci owned the next one in the family, named Little Beagle. As the President explained at the time, "It's cheaper if we all have the same monogram." Little Beagle grew to be just plain Beagle, a pleasant dog with great soulful eyes and an affectionate disposition, and for fifteen years, Beagle was very dear to the Senator, and became his dog. In 1955 when he suffered a heart attack, he was in a depressed mood. Always active physically as well as politically, the enforced idleness was almost unendurable. When Mr. Johnson's spirits were lowest, Beagle understood what he needed. He would climb up on the bed and stretch out beside the patient, his face snuggled alongside his master's. Mr. Johnson always said that the dog saw him safely through the worst weeks of his illness. When Beagle died of old age, he was buried in a special plot of ground on the LBJ ranch.

The two beagles of White House days were taken from the same litter, born during the summer of 1963. They were presented to Luci Johnson by Mr. Willard Deasons, a close friend of the First Family. Luci, showing the same simple directness as her father, named the pups Him and Her. Frisky, sniffing curiously at everybody and everything that crossed their paths, the beagle pups turned the White House lawn into their private playground. As they nipped at each other, rolling around and doing the things that normal, healthy dogs do, the President found them delightful.

Soon another dog arrived at the White House, one that reminded veteran capital observers of the Coolidge pets. Just before Christmas, 1963, nine-year-old Lois Nelson of Woodstock, Illinois, presented the President with a six-month-old white collie, which Mr. Johnson accepted as a gift from all the children in the United States. He was named Blanco, probably because that was the name of a small town in Texas near the Johnson ranch, and also because Blanco is the Spanish word for white.

Blanco was indeed a rare one. Supposedly there were only about a dozen pure white collies in the country. Perhaps because of some inbred defect, many are born deaf. Blanco's hearing was normal, but he was timid and nervous. In order to keep his silky coat spotless, Blanco was bathed every four or five days.

Him, Her, and Blanco got along about as well as any dogs can. They ate together and slept together. Each was provided with a mat tacked onto sponge rubber pads. Being pups they chewed up several sets of bedding, shredding the mats gleefully one after the other. Their accommodations were in a room near the Flower Room.

Very seldom did Mr. Johnson fail to stop and look in on his dogs. If he didn't see them in the morning, he would take a five-minute break from his strenuous schedule sometime during the day to play with the pups. This was his time for relaxation and nothing was allowed to interfere with it. Before the short romp he would reach into his desk drawer for a bottle of candy-coated vitamin pills —each dog was fed two pills a day—and then he would step outside. A short piercing whistle, and the two beagles and the collie would show up, making a mad dash for "the Boss," each determined to get the first pat on the head.

If the weather was inclement, the President would pick up the telephone and call Mr. Traphes Bryant, the combination White House electrician and major domo of the animals, a post he had also filled for the Kennedys.

"Please bring the dogs," Mr. Johnson would say, and they would be ushered into the office for a few moments of frolic.

Soon the dogs became very much a part of the President's daily routine. When he left on a trip, he expected the dogs to be present to see him off, as he helicoptered up and away. When he returned, he would peer out the window of the hovering chopper to see if the dogs were there to greet him. They always were.

Luci was not cut off completely from the dogs. During an illness Mrs. Johnson surprised her by bringing Him and Her for a short visit. But by then, Luci was quite aware that they were attached to her father.

It was during an informal conference that President Johnson made his great mistake with the beagles. He was strolling about the lawn with several bankers discussing with them the gap in our balance of foreign trade payments. The President stopped, took out the candy vitamins and fed them to the dogs. Then taking Him by the ears, he pulled the beagle up so he stood up on his hind legs. Him let loose a loud yelp. The bankers, watching, expressed surprise at the way the President handled the dog. Mr. Johnson replied that "it was good for Him," adding that all beagle hound owners liked to hear their dogs bark. Then he repeated the ear pulling with Her, who also yelped. Several newspaper reporters and photographers were present. The next day the story was in print, and the flap that followed caused the President's own ears to burn. Tons of letters and telegrams tidal-waved into the White House and the ASPCA, as dog owners all over the country shook their fists at Mr. Johnson, literally and in writing. Never before had there been such a storm of protest over the action of a President with his pet. How so many people had so little to do that they could write letters like this I'll never understand. Mr. Johnson was bewildered at the fuss. Everybody knew he wasn't a cruel man. Neither were his friends who also owned beagle hounds, and they pulled their dogs' ears once in a while for the same reason he did. The beagles still loved him as much as ever, and he doted on them. Nevertheless, it toook a long time before the President was able to emerge from the doghouse of his own making.

A sly partisan note was introduced by Senate Majority Leader Everett Dirksen at one of his news conferences. Asked what he thought of the incident, the honey-voiced Illinois patriarch said he didn't want to get involved in the to-do because it happened to a "Democratic dog."

Her was a little more than one year old when she died, on November 27, 1964. While nosing around the lawn she picked up and swallowed a small rock. The playful beagle expired on the operating table. For the President that was a woeful day. Although he tried never to express a preference for one dog over the other, he confided that Her had a sweeter disposition than Him, the latter being somewhat independent and stubborn at times.

It seems that the President never loved Blanco quite as much as he did the beagles, no doubt because of his great affection for the beagle he had earlier. But he never treated Blanco any differently from Him. The President continued to stop by for a chat and a pat with the two remaining dogs.

Blanco and Him were numbers one and two of Washington's "Top Ten Dogs." At least they were so rated according to the numbers on their license tags, and a low dog-license number was a greater status symbol in Washington than an exclusive automobile license plate. Records for 1965 indicate that Him had dog license number one and Blanco was issued number two. The other eight included: George, a poodle owned by Engineer Commissioner Charles M. Duke; Buttons, a poodle belonging to Mrs. Martha Donohue; Chhota S., Frederick J. Clark's poodle; G. Boy and Cindy, two cairns owned by F.B.I. chief J. Edgar Hoover; Jonah, Mr. Duncan Ransdell's chihuahua; Ginger Boy, a chihuahua owned by Norman Bowles, Jr.; and Beau, the poodle belonging to General Omar N. Bradley. Evidently all the other dogs were also-rans.

Soon there were more beagles at the White House. Him fathered a litter, the mother being a Delaware beagle. The new dog names heard around the Executive Mansion included Kim, Freckles, Edgar, Dumpling, and Little Chap.

After a while, most of them were given away, and only Kim and Freckles remained at the White House.

This led to a misunderstanding when new license tags were issued, and the scramble for Top Ten leadership was renewed. (I'm not sure whether this is hilarious or ridiculous—maybe both. But to me it's really ridiculous.) New license tags were issued to the White House dogs. This time Blanco was relegated to the number four spot. The President had not intended to treat the collie in this shabby fashion. For no other reason than longevity, he was still entitled to the second-place position.

The error was traced to a gardener who received a call asking how many tags the President needed. He replied that four were required, one for Him, two for the beagle pups, and one for Blanco. The city issued the tags in that order. Dropped from the list were the dogs belonging to Mr. Norman Bowles and General Bradley.

Him and Blanco continued to play together, nipping and nudging each other in fun, although sometimes they went at it for real. It wasn't clear how it happened, and perhaps Blanco did it, but Him received a bite on the eye that sent him to the hospital. The cut was on the edge of the eye and healed. Just an inch more to the center and Him might have been half blinded. The President remarked that if Him and Blanco ever had a real knockdown, drag-out fight, he thought Him would win, but he never let the growling get too far out of hand.

In July 1966, Him died. The frisky beagle had always

liked to chase squirrels. He spotted one and went yipping after it. The squirrel got away, but Him ran between the wheels of a White House car and was struck and killed instantly. Mrs. Johnson was in Lincoln, Nebraska, when she heard the news. Shaking her head, she said, "That makes you feel like you've been hit in the stomach by a hard rock." The President with a strained look on his face, said quietly, "It's a sad night tonight at the White House."

And then Yuki arrived!

Luci and her husband were at a gas station in Austin, Texas, when they saw a lonesome-looking pooch wandering aimlessly around. Nobody knew who he belonged to, so the newlyweds took him home. The mongrel's quick, alert manner soon melted the President.

Yuki was given the run of the White House, and that included living rooms, dining rooms, bedrooms, and most of the time the President's Oval Office. He was able to make the acquaintance of kings and ambassadors, with or without formal introduction. Yuki shared the President in conference and also had him all to himself. He would sit under the table at Cabinet meetings. Yuki was a very well-behaved dog according to various men who attended these meetings.

Why did President Lyndon B. Johnson show such partiality for a dog with absolutely no pedigree, no traceable lineage, a homeless vagabond? Mr. Johnson gave two reasons: First, "He speaks with a Texas accent." Second, and even more important, "Because he likes me."

One of the last official acts of Mr. Johnson as he left the White House was to make sure that Yuki was taken by helicopter to Andrews Air Force Base outside Washington to wait for the President and the other members of the family. Together they were all going home to Texas on Air Force One.

Chapter 14

OLD WHITEY

THE story is told of a young second lieutenant, fresh from the great, gray walls of West Point, who approached a grizzled, weary disreputable-looking man and began his conversation with, "Say, old codger..." Only later did he discover that the ancient warrior was, in fact, his commanding officer, General Zachary Taylor! When the lieutenant tried to stammer an apology, he was told, "Never judge a stranger by his clothes."

The lieutenant had made a perfectly natural mistake. At first glance, General Taylor looked more like a camp follower than the leader of an army. His uniform was screamingly non-regulation and ill-fitting. His coat was shapeless, his boots dirty, his hat picked up heaven only knows where. It wasn't that General Taylor was unaware of his appearance, it's just that he didn't care. The general's bearing was equally unmilitary. In the midst of a battle with shots whining dangerously close, he could be seen mounted on his horse, one leg slung carelessly over the pommel, peering intently at the action through the smoky haze.

Any description of General Taylor may sound uncharitable at best. His large head was completely out of proportion with the rest of his body. He had a large nose set into a rather homely face, with thin lips and piercing eyes. Under his thick neck was a bulky torso, and legs so short that an orderly had to help him get on his horse.

Zachary Taylor was commissioned as an officer by President Thomas Jefferson when Taylor was only twenty-four years old. He became increasingly careless about his uniform as he rose to higher rank. He felt that a man in the Army was either a fashion plate or a soldier, and he chose the latter.

His battle charger mirrored him completely. Old Whitey was a grayish-white, shaggy-maned, knock-kneed, uncurried steed, of a type most often described as a "family horse." It is doubtful that his mane or hide ever felt a brush or currycomb. In manner, the horse appeared placid, almost to the point of lethargy. Only one thing could excite him, and that was a parade. When the general reviewed his troops and when the band began to play, Old Whitey seemed to come to life. His head would toss, his hooves would paw the ground, and up came the head proudly. He didn't walk; he pranced. And almost in time with the music.

To Americans reading eagerly of the exploits of the Mexican campaign, the general was far larger than life, a towering figure, a genuine homespun hero. Old Whitey became the most famous horse in the United States. No battle, however savage, seemed to perturb this seedy-looking, scraggly steed. Rider and mount would stand atop a hill in plain sight of enemy sharpshooters and cannoneers, distressingly close to the action.

On one occasion, a shell burst only a few yards away. On another General Taylor's uniform was twice pierced by rifle bullets across the chest and through the sleeves. When the general got into the thick of front-line fighting, firing his pistol and crouching alongside his infantry, there was Old Whitey, examining the ground to see if there might not be a blade or two of grass worth munching. The bravery of both was incredible, yet miraculously, both emerged without harm.

Old Whitey carried General Taylor through hundreds of miles in the Mexican War from the battle of Palo Alto, Texas, to the tough fighting at Monterey and on to the bitter end in Buena Vista. Old Whitey with Old Rough n' Ready on his back became a familiar sight to the troops as they marched at the head of the column or dashed back to the rear to check on stragglers. Sometimes General Taylor dismounted so that Whitey could help drag a heavy gun up the steep slope.

When might fell and the soldiers stopped to bivouac, Old Whitey would be unsaddled and left to graze outside the general's camp. Orderlies coddled this beat-up, scraggly mount. They patted his rump, stroked his muzzle, gave him such stray goodies as could be scrounged up on a long hot march. To the troops, Old Whitey was as much their horse as Zachary Taylor was their chief. Neither could do wrong in their eyes.

General Taylor and Old Whitey received a hero's welcome upon their return to the United States. From the time they disembarked at New Orleans and through the trip to Baton Rouge, every day was a holiday. Cannons were fired, bugles blared, the band played, and the journey was one long parade through flower-strewn streets. Old Whitey was truly in his element.

It has been said that no man has the necessary training to become President of the United States. But Zachary Taylor perhaps had less to recommend him for the job than other candidates. He had little schooling and no knowledge of government or politics. Taylor had never voted on anything. He was simply a regular Army man, the first such to become President.

Other Chief Executives had been Army officers, but they had really been "citizen soldiers." Soldiering was the only life Zachary Taylor had ever known. However, his magnetism as a war hero was such that the Whigs astutely realized he was unbeatable.

There is one interesting oddity concerning the Presidency itself that took place immediately prior to President Taylor's taking the oath of office. President James Polk's Administration officially expired on Sunday, March 4, 1849, promptly at 12 noon. Vice President George Mifflin Dallas had resigned his post as President of the Senate on March 2, and, like President Polk, he too was out of office March 4. In order to have a head of Senate, Senator David Rice Atchison was elected President of the Senate *pro tempore* on March 2. He kept this office through March 3, and was re-elected on March 5, so that he could administer the oath of office to the incoming Chief Executive. According to Article Two of the Constitution, should the President be unable to serve for the reasons enumerated, the office is passed on to the Vice President. But there was no such official, at least on Sunday afternoon. The closest thing the country had to a Vice President was Senator David Atchison who was President *pro tem* of the Senate.

There are a number of legal minds who insist that although he was never elected to the office, Senator Atchison was President of the United States for one day!

President Zachary Taylor was a fish out of water in the White House. Politics was a game beyond his mastery. Ethics and honor were strangers to Washington, but these were the creed of a soldier, and the only way he had been trained to act. There was only one stable, unchanging thing in his life—the sight of Old Whitey grazing peacefully on the White House lawn. The faithful old charger was as much beloved as ever. Visitors, seeking souvenirs, helped themselves to a hair from Whitey's tail. He was fed sugar lumps and tender carrots. Whitey was nuzzled and patted by admiring ladies.

He took it all with the greatest aplomb. As long as his

master came over to him from time to time for a brief chat, then all was right with the world.

In spite of all the attention he received, Old Whitey continued to look as unkempt as ever. Undoubtedly the stable hands did what they could to make him look presentable. Senator William Seward of New York even presented the horse with a silver comb. Nothing seemed to help. Even as some men seem to look unpressed even in suits just returned from the cleaners, so Whitey looked shaggy. He had grown old by then.

However, if anything even faintly resembled a parade, Whitey was there and he wanted in. When New York City's Phoenix Hook and Ladder Company paid the President a visit, the uniformed firemen struck up an air as they marched across the White House grounds. Nothing loath, to the President's amusement, Whitey edged into the procession, looking for a convenient space. To the horse, martial music meant parades, and if he wanted to join in, what was wrong with that?

Usually Whitey had the freedom of the grounds. If people were wandering about the lawns, he would join them in the friendliest way. Only when the Marine band gave its Sunday concert on the grounds was Whitey tethered. The President never knew when his wartime friend might nose in among the musicians, wondering when the parade was going to start.

July 4, 1850, was a hot, humid day. President Taylor had attended some ceremonies and returned home, very

tired after a long afternoon in the sun. To refresh himself
he ate some cherries and drank ice cold milk. Soon afterwards he became very ill. Attending physicians thought
it might be cholera. Whatever the illness was, in five days
he was dead. Old Whitey was standing under the President's window the night the bell tolled, the bell on the
top of the Department of State. There was much hurrying
and scurrying about, but the old charger paid it no mind
as he continued to browse, nibbling here and there at the
sweet clover. On July 12, the President's body lay in state.
The next morning, after services, the long, sad processional
began its journey toward Congress Cemetery.

Close behind the casket marching in his final parade
was Old Whitey, with holsters and reverse boots on his
saddle. As tears came down their cheeks, people bade
farewell to both, for they knew the heroic charger's days
in Washington were also at an end. But Old Whitey
seemed to be reliving the glory of days long gone. As
cannons boomed, as bells tolled, as mournful music was
played, Whitey, sometimes with head bowed, or on occasion swishing his scraggly tail, followed the President of
the United States to his final resting place.

Chapter 15

MORE PETS THAN KENNEDYS

THAT Caroline Kennedy was pet-oriented from the time she could walk was best evidenced by her meeting with John Glenn, first American to orbit the earth. The little girl had been filled in on previous space shots attempted by the United States, including one that had as capsule passenger a chimp named Enos. That must have been the one that impressed her the most, for when she was presented to Astronaut Glenn, Caroline instantly inquired, "Where's the monkey?"

The Kennedy children came by their love for animals honestly. The President's family had a number of dogs and other pets, but it was Jacqueline Kennedy who influenced them most. Mrs. Kennedy had practically grown up with horses and dogs, and indeed, had raised her own 4-H calf. She introduced them to pets when they were barely more than infants. Caroline received a Welsh terrier named Charlie when she was only one year old.

When the new First Family was settled in the White

House, an animal nose count would have included the dog, Charlie; a cat named Tom Kitten; a canary named Robin; a couple of parakeets answering to the names of Bluebelle and Maybelle; a crazy assortment of hamsters who were always discovering new ways to get themselves killed; two ponies, Macaroni and Leprechaun, soon joined by a third named Tex, a gift of Lyndon B. Johnson.

Time, attrition, and grisly traits thinned out the ranks somewhat, but reinforcements always filled out the animal regiment sooner or later.

Tom Kitten grew progressively more morose and meowly and finally, to make him happier and also to get him away from the President (he was always in the President's room, and the President was allergic to animal fur), Mrs. Kennedy decided to give him to her secretary, Mrs. Mary Gallagher, who had two young children. Caroline took the news and the explanation gracefully. She was very pleased to learn that Tom later married another feline known only as Mother Cat. Tom Kitten by this time, being a boy's cat, was called Tom Terrific.

Robin, the canary, died and was buried with much pomp and ceremony on the South Lawn. Two days later, the Shah and Empress of Iran arrived on a visit of state. The Empress met Caroline and her playschool friends. The children bowed and curtsied and formally presented her with daffodils and a batch of crayon drawings which the Empress gravely accepted with thanks. As the two First Ladies were leaving on a White House tour, Caroline

called out, "Mother, be sure to show her Robin's grave."
Off they went to the South Lawn, accompanied, at a re-
spectful distance, by Macaroni.

The hamsters seemed bent on suicide or murder and
often succeeded in accomplishing both. Once, a few of
them got into the President's bathtub and one drowned.
It is an enormous tub. Then hamsters Debbie and Billy
became parents to six children. Billy suddenly devoured
them all, whereupon the enraged Debbie attacked and
killed Billy. Then she saddened, sickened, and also died.
Caroline could never understand why that happened.
Neither can I. They certainly must have been a bunch of
neurotics.

Macaroni stoicly endured the bouncing of Caroline and
John, Jr. Mrs. Kennedy wanted her children to learn to
ride well. She herself was one of the most accomplished
horsewomen in White House history. Furthermore, the
First Lady told Caroline and John that when they were
old enough, she would teach them to feed, groom, and
saddle their own horses. Caroline became a first-rate
equestrienne. John, Jr., got his first ride when only fifteen
months old, with Mrs. Kennedy walking alongside, keeping him erect on the saddle. All he said was, "I wanna
get off."

Truth to tell, the pony liked all the Kennedys and longed
to be around them. One afternoon, while working at his
desk, the President looked up to find Macaroni peering in
at him through the window. President and pony stared at

each other thoughtfully for a moment or two; then Mr. Kennedy grinned, opened the door, and invited the pony inside. Instead of accepting, Macaroni turned and went away. He thus missed the immortality of becoming the first horse ever to walk into a President's office.

In a number of respects, the gift pets received by the Kennedys were individually more unusual than those received by preceding First Families. Probably some people thought that those fresh young White House residents with a marvelous sense of humor might just like them well enough to keep them. In his book, *With Kennedy,* Press Secretary Pierre Salinger described the arrival of a rabbit who played a toy trumpet and enjoyed drinking beer. The bunny, sent by a magician, was named Zsa Zsa. When reporters asked Mr. Salinger about the new pet, he responded in his usual impish manner. The reporter asked, "Mr. Secretary, do you know if this rabbit is a lush?"

Answer: "All I know about Zsa Zsa is that she is supposed to be able to play the first five bars of the Star-Spangled Banner on a toy golden trumpet."

Reporter: "Could we have the rabbit come over here and run through a couple of numbers for us?"

Salinger: "I can ask her."

Reporter: "Was the rabbit playing this trumpet as it came into the White House?"

Salinger: "No. The trumpet came under separate cover and will be sent to the orphanage with the rabbit. I don't think Zsa Zsa should be without her trumpet."

Reporter: "You're not sending her to the orphanage?"
Salinger: "Immediately." *

After Mrs. Kennedy's state visit to Pakistan, President Mohammed Ayub Khan sent her a gorgeous bay gelding named Sardar, plus an offer of an elephant and a few tiger cubs. As one who appreciated outstanding horses— and Sardar certainly was that—the First Lady was more than pleased to have him. But she politely declined the elephant and cubs.

There were dogs aplenty arriving all the time. Charlie was joined by Clipper, a German shepherd sent by the President's father; Shannon, an Irish cocker, the gift of Prime Minister Eamon de Valera of Ireland; a huge wolfhound, appropriately named Wolf, which was the gift of a Dublin priest by the name of Kennedy. This animal was described as a dog who didn't like other dogs. And then there was Pushinka.

All the Kennedys smiled at the six-month-old fluffy white dog, but the one who fell head over heels in love with her was Caroline's dog, Charlie. Pushinka had a rather tough beginning. She had to overcome several obstacles before she won acceptance, for she was a gift from Nikita Khrushchev, the top man of the Soviet Union. In truth, Premier Khrushchev was bestowing a rare gift on Caroline, for Pushinka was the daughter of Strelka, the

* Pierre Salinger, *With Kennedy* (New York: Doubleday, 1966). Copyright © 1966 by Pierre Salinger. Reprinted by permission of Doubleday & Company, Inc.

first Russian orbiting space-dog, and Pushok, a dog who had been used in many Soviet ground experiments.

A few silly people objected to Pushinka's presence, declaring that anything coming from the Soviet Union was Communist, even a dog. How nutty can you get?

Pushinka—the name was very appropriate, as in Russian it means "fluffy"—was given a physical examination at Walter Reed Hospital. In fact, this processing took so long that the Army and the White House were forced to issue a series of denials that Pushinka harbored mysterious germs, capable of starting a terrible plague, or that Pushinka had come equipped with a mini-transmitter planted inside her body so that she could be used to bug secret meetings.

Perhaps it was a combination of Pushinka's shy good looks and her scientific-minded parents that caused Charlie to flip his wig over the Russian charmer. Charlie himself could boast only vague lineal relationship to a dog named Asta, who had made quite a name for himself in a series of movies in the 1930s called "The Thin Man," which starred William Powell and Myrna Loy.

The union of Charlie and Pushinka was blessed with four little pups: Butterfly, White Tips, Blackie, and Steaker. One of them was given to the Lawfords, the President's sister and her husband, the movie actor. A letter-writing contest for children was used to dispose of two more dogs. In order to win the dog, the youngster had to describe the type of home and the care a dog should get. More than ten thousand letters were received.

One of the best didn't win because the sender forgot to include his name and address. It read: "I will raise the dog to be a Democrat and bite all Republicans."

There were always more than enough pets to go around at the White House, but if things ever got dull, Caroline and John, Jr., could always drop in on Uncle Bobby who didn't live too far away. Local capital "wits" used the shopworn but true joke that the army of Kennedy kids were outnumbered only by the bigger army of Kennedy kids' pets. Even a computer working overtime couldn't begin to enumerate the variety and numbers of animals comprising the clan's private zoo, scattered all around of course, not all at the White House. A fast roll call might list about three dozen rabbits, seven or so ponies, a horse and a donkey, over a dozen assorted hens, roosters, geese, pigeons, tanks full of goldfish and tadpoles, a burro, two cockatoos and a parakeet, a pair of Angora goats, a tortoise, maybe six or seven turtles—and a guinea pig named Crooked Coconut, the special private property of Robert Kennedy, Jr. Bobby the younger also went visiting his Uncle Jack to show him a new salamander named Shadrack, which was discussed and examined at great length. Reportedly, the President agreed that it was an excellent salamander.

And through this barrage of animals strode President Kennedy, a perpetually bemused look on his face, as if wondering how he got himself into such a predicament. He suffered with Caroline when Pushinka ran away and rejoiced with her when the dog was found. He laughed with his wife and children when walking through the nursery, a parakeet would swoop down and roost atop his head.

Overwhelmed with such problems as the Cuban missile crisis, the war in Vietnam, the Alliance for Progress, the Berlin Wall, the Test Ban treaty, or anything else that seemed to defy solution, he found his own temporary surcease. He would just step briskly onto the lawn outside his office and clap his hands. Within seconds, dogs, let out of the kennels, and children of Caroline's playschool would come running from behind fences and atop slides. They would converge on him, making the kind of racket only a young father can know and understand. He would stand in their midst, grinning his famous grin, watching them play or ride the pony.

There was a birthday party at the White House once for Caroline and John-John. It was visited by a monkey named Suzy, all dressed up in a dress. Suzy apparently came from the Baltimore zoo to do tricks for the children and she ran around, eating with them and shrieking with them. Suzy stole the show, and Mrs. Kennedy didn't particularly care for the publicity that Suzy got in the newspapers. I don't blame her. So after that there was no more Suzy at birthday parties.

All in all, the Kennedy family made good use of the

White House. It's a marvelous place for children—young children—to run and shriek and ride a pony, play with dogs, cats, hamsters. They ranged over the whole house and the enormous grounds. Even in the playschool, in the solarium on the third floor or on the roof over the Truman balcony, the children could raise rabbits and ride their bicycles.

Children don't have to worry about the bigger problems faced by the President, but he could take enormous delight in watching their pleasure in playing with their pets.

Chapter 16

JEFFERSON AND MADISON

If "pets" can include all animals that are treated in a friendly manner by our Presidents, then Thomas Jefferson might be considered in this the leader of all Chief Executives. On the grounds of his Monticello estate he allowed all creatures to live in peace except those that preyed on others. In the shelter of his woods lived deer, rabbit, peacock, guinea hens, wild poultry, pigeons, squirrels, pheasants, and partridges. All sought the asylum of Mr. Jefferson's forest. He also had a fish pond, where he captured trout alive. Most of the time the fish were spared only until dinner. Thomas Jefferson trained a mockingbird, and the bird made a pleasant companion for the widowed President.

He was something of a home workshop hobbyist, as well as an indoor gardener, and had fixed up the ground floor of the White House to his liking. Wall maps, bookcases, and a large table were in one room. The cabinets and drawers held his hammers and saws, his garden tools, and a variety of potted plants and flowers.

This indoor garden area was ideal for keeping his mockingbird in homelike surroundings. President Jefferson's bird spent a great deal of time outside of the cage. He taught it a great many tricks such as pecking out bits of fruit from between his lips. Mr. Jefferson was a good amateur violinist and sometimes he did a duet with his feathered friend, the President playing a tune, the mockingbird whistling. The bird would amuse the President by imitating the calls of other birds or sometimes even sounds similar to those of a dog or a cat.

When President James Madison took office in 1809, Washington, D.C., was a thriving community of some eight thousand people. But to the ministers coming from the populated capitals of France, England, and other foreign lands, the American center of government was provincial. When widower Thomas Jefferson entertained, he did so neither lavishly nor often. When he did have a dinner or party, he asked Dolley Madison, the wife of James Madison, his Secretary of State, to help him entertain guests. In that way, Mrs. Madison became a great friend of President Jefferson's mockingbird. Probably she was more appreciative than most of the bird's great charm, for she herself was a proud owner of an intelligent talking parrot.

Dolley Madison, as First Lady, had her own ideas of what a party should be like. Many times it took the form of a buffet, with huge platters of Virginia ham, corn, relishes, and other hearty dishes. Some foreign visitors who attended some of the welcoming parties remarked that it seemed to be "more like a harvest-home supper than the entertainment of the Secretary of State." Mrs. Madison replied sweetly that such amounts of food were the results of "the happy circumstances of the super-abundance and prosperity of our country." And she would add that it was her policy to "sacrifice a delicacy in European tastes for the less elegant but more liberal fashion of Virginia." Her larder and wine cellar were always well stocked.

At Mrs. Madison's gatherings her parrot was always the star attraction. Parrots were not numerous in the new city of Washington, and Dolley's bird was something of a novelty. Youngsters especially were enamored of the parrot. The President and his wife had no children of their own; Mrs. Madison's son by an earlier marriage was away at school. However, Dolley's sister, Anna, also lived in Washington and was married to Congressman Richard Cutts. There were three nephews and a niece constantly visiting at the Executive Mansion. Richard, Jr., Walter, James Madison Cutts, and the First Lady's namesake, Dolley Cutts.

In order to play the children's favorite game, Mrs. Madison would open the parrot's cage and the bird would hop out, fly down to the floor, and begin to peck away at little Dolley's feet. Finishing the toes, the parrot would seek out Master James's shoebuckles and rap on them a few times. In turn all the children would receive a tweek, a tug, or a peck from the green bird that never failed to elicit shrieks of delight.

During the War of 1812 it became apparent that the city of Washington would be too difficult to defend. The British Fleet Commander, Admiral Cockburn, boasted that he would soon be sitting "in Dolley's parlor," and in time he made good that bit of bluster. The American troops were defeated at Bladensburg and the path to the capital lay open, undefended. President Madison, who had been with the troops at Bladensburg, sent his wife a hastily penciled note directing her to get out of the city with all possible haste, but to save the Cabinet papers.

Mrs. Madison obeyed, and as she soon wrote: "I have pressed as many Cabinet papers [this included the Declaration of Independence] into trunks as to fill my carriage," as well as a wagon "filled with plate." The precious portrait of George Washington painted by Gilbert Stuart she "placed in the hands of two gentlemen of New York for safekeeping."

As she departed, Madison asked one of the servants, Jean Sioussat, who was commonly called French John, to take care of the parrot. The streets of Washington were jammed with people fleeing from the red coats. Some of these "good citizens" (described by aide Paul Jennings as a rabble) took advantage of the milling and confusion, entering the executive house, running through the rooms to steal whatever was not nailed to the floors.

Before burning the house, the invading British also helped themselves to wine and provisions from the well-stocked larder.

As for French John, he took the parrot to the Octagon House, a residence owned by Colonel Benjamin Tayloe. The parrot was given to the cook for safekeeping. After the British departed, the bird was retrieved and returned to his mistress.

For about a year, the Madisons and their pet lived in Octagon House, one of the most beautiful houses in Washington. There were no iron bars around the house and neighborhood children found it convenient and exciting to drop in on the First Lady or stand outside the window to get a glimpse of her fabulous bird. Mrs. Madison never failed to put the bird through its paces.

The parrot lived for a long time. President Madison died in 1836, and the parrot was alive at the time. When Mrs. Madison reached her seventieth birthday, it was reported that she was still being amused by her pet. Parrots are known to be very long-lived, and it is possible that this one outlived Dolley herself. A famous old lady, she moved from the Madison estate in Montpelier in Virginia back to the capital where she lived past her eighty-first birthday.

CALENDAR OF PRESIDENTIAL
FAMILY PETS

President's Pets	Date of Inauguration
GEORGE WASHINGTON	1789

Samson, Steady, Leonidas, Traveller, Magnolia, and other stallions

Nelson and Blueskin, horses used during the Revolution

Horse given to Washington by General Braddock

Mopsey, Taster, Cloe, Tipler, Forester, Captain, Lady, Rover Vulcan, Sweetlips, and Searcher, all hounds; and five French hounds

Rozinante, Nellie Custis' horse

Parrot belonging to Martha Washington

THOMAS JEFFERSON	1801

Mockingbird

JAMES MADISON	1809

Green parrot belonging to Dolley Madison

JAMES MONROE	1817

Spaniel belonging to Maria Monroe

JOHN QUINCY ADAMS	1825

Alligator belonging to Lafayette

Silkworms belonging to Mrs. Adams

ANDREW JACKSON	1829

Sam Patches, wartime mount

Emily, Lady Nashville, and Bolivia, racing fillies

President's Pets (cont'd)	Date of Inauguration
Truxton, champion race horse	
Other ponies	
MARTIN VAN BUREN	1837
Two tiger cubs	
WILLIAM HENRY HARRISON	1841
Billy goat	
Durham cow	
JOHN TYLER	1841
The General, a horse	
ZACHARY TAYLOR	1849
Old Whitey, wartime mount	
ABRAHAM LINCOLN	1861
Pig, childhood pet	
Fido, family dog	
Ponies belonging to Tad and Willy Lincoln	
White rabbit	
Nanny and Nanko, Tad Lincoln's goats	
Jack, Tad Lincoln's turkey	
Jip, Lincoln's dog	
Also: cats and dogs	
ANDREW JOHNSON	1865
Pet mice	
ULYSSES S. GRANT	1869
Jeff Davis, wartime mount	
Cincinnatus, saddle horse	
Egypt and St. Louis, carriage horses	
Julia, racer	
Reb and Billy Button, Shetland ponies	
Jennie and Mary, Nellie Grant's mares	
Butcher Boy, horse	

	Date of
President's Pets (cont'd)	Inauguration

Parrot belonging to Jesse Grant
Gamecocks belonging to Jesse Grant
Faithful, Jesse Grant's Newfoundland
Also: other dogs

RUTHERFORD HAYES   1877
Pedigreed Jersey cows
Carriage horses
Scott's goats and dogs

JAMES GARFIELD   1881
Kit, Molly Garfield's mare

GROVER CLEVELAND   1885
Canaries and mockingbirds belonging to Mrs. Cleveland
Japanese poodle

BENJAMIN HARRISON   1889
Dogs and billy goat belonging to grandchildren

WILLIAM MCKINLEY   1897
Mexican double-yellow-headed parrot

THEODORE ROOSEVELT   1901
Bleistein, Roosevelt's favorite horse
Renown, Roswell, Rusty, Jocko, Root, Grey Dawn, Wyoming, and Yagenka, all horses
General and Judge, carriage horses
Algonquin, Archie Roosevelt's calico pony
Pete, bull terrier
Sailor Boy, Chesapeake retriever
Jack, Kermit Roosevelt's terrier
Skip, a mongrel
Manchu, Alice Roosevelt's spaniel
Emily Spinach, Alice Roosevelt's snake

President's Pets (cont'd)

Snakes belonging to Quentin Roosevelt
Tom Quartz, cat
Slippers, cat
Josiah, badger
Dewey Senior, Dewey Junior, Bob Evans, Bishop
  Doan, and Father O'Grady, all guinea pigs
Also: lion, hyena, wildcat, coyote, five bears, two par-
  rots, zebra, barn owl, snakes, lizards, rats, roosters,
  raccoon

WILLIAM TAFT   1909
Pauline Wayne, last cow at the White House

WOODROW WILSON   1913
Old Ike, the tobacco-chewing ram
Sheep

WARREN HARDING   1921
Laddie Boy, Airedale
Oh Boy, bulldog
Canaries belonging to Mrs. Harding

CALVIN COOLIDGE   1923
Peter Pan, terrier
Paul Pry, Airedale, originally named Laddie Buck
Rob Roy, white collie, originally named Oshkosh
Prudence Prim, white collie
Calamity Jane, Shetland sheepdog
Tiny Tim, chow
Blackberry, chow
Ruby Rough, brown collie
Boston Beans, bulldog
King Kole, police dog
Bessie, yellow collie
Palo Alto, bird dog

President's Pets (cont'd)

Nip and Tuck, canaries
Snowflake, white canary
Old Bill, thrush
Enoch, goose
Mockingbird belonging to Mrs. Coolidge
Tiger, alley cat
Blacky, cat
Rebecca and Horace, raccoons
Ebenezer, donkey
Smokey, bobcat
Also: lion cubs, wallaby, pigmy hippo, bear

HERBERT HOOVER   1929
King Tut, police dog
Big Ben and Sonnie, fox terriers
Glen, Scotch collie
Yukon, Eskimo dog
Patrick, wolfhound
Eaglehurst Gillette, sitter
Weejie, elkhound
Pat, police dog

FRANKLIN DELANO ROOSEVELT   1933
Major, German shepherd
Meggie, Scotch terrier
Winks, Llewellyn setter
Tiny, English sheepdog
President, Great Dane
Fala, Scotch terrier
Blaze, Elliot Roosevelt's mastiff

HARRY S. TRUMAN   1945
Feller, the unwanted dog
Mike, Margaret Truman's Irish setter

President's Pets (cont'd)	Date of Inauguration
DWIGHT D. EISENHOWER	1953

Heidi, Weimaraner

JOHN F. KENNEDY   1961
Charlie, Caroline Kennedy's Welsh terrier
Tom Kitten, cat
Robin, canary
Bluebell and Maybelle, parakeets
Macaroni, Caroline Kennedy's pony
Tex and Leprechaun, ponies
Debbie and Billie, hamsters
Pushinka, Shannon, Wolf, and Clipper, dogs
Butterfly, White Tips, Blackie, and Streaker, Pushinka
   and Charlie's pups
Zsa Zsa, rabbit
Sardar, Mrs. Kennedy's horse

LYNDON B. JOHNSON   1963
Beagle and Little Beagle
Him and Her, beagles
Blanco, white collie
Yuki, mongrel
Hamsters and lovebirds

RICHARD NIXON   1969
Vicky, poodle
Pasha, terrier
King Timahoe, Irish setter